P9-DFV-600

BREAKING UP, DOWN AND THROUGH

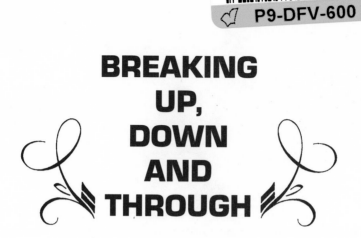

Discovering
Spiritual and Psychological Opportunities
in Your Transitions

Andre Papineau

Paulist Press
New York / Mahwah, N.J.

Cover design by Kathy McKeen.

Copyright © 1997 by Rev. Andre Papineau

All rights reserved. No part of this book may be reproduced or trans-
mitted in any form or by any means, electronic or mechanical, including photocopying, recording or by any information storage and
retrieval system without permission in writing from the Publisher.

Library of Congress Cataloging-in-Publication Data

Papineau, Andre, 1937–
    Breaking up, down and through : discovering spiritual and psy-
chological opportunities in your transitions / Andre Papineau.
        p.   cm.
    Includes bibliographical references.
    ISBN 0-8091-3715-1 (alk. paper)
    1. Change (Psychology)   2. Change (Psychology)—Religious
aspects. 3. Adjustment (Psychology) 4. Adjustment (Psychology)—
Religious aspects. I. Title.
BF637.C4P36   1997
155.2′4—dc21   97-15032
                                                                      CIP

Published by Paulist Press
997 Macarthur Boulevard
Mahwah, New Jersey 07430

Printed and bound in the
United States of America

BF
637
.C4
P36
1997

Contents

Acknowledgments

I am deeply indebted to Dan Pekarshe for his invaluable assistance and encouragement in writing this book. And I am especially grateful for his friendship. I would also like to express my appreciation to my friend, Richard Kenyon, for his helpful suggestions.

Introduction

The message of this book is simple. It is okay not to feel okay when going through a transition. Convincing ourselves and others of this won't be easy. Our language is replete with the rhetoric of fulfillment. We are exhorted by the media to be self-actualized and well-adjusted. We are encouraged to be whole, happy human beings who ought to be getting to ever higher planes or discovering an ever higher self.

To achieve these goals we need to realize our potential, discover our true selves, contact our inner child, and meditate on our mantra. Once we have done all of this, we can feel good about ourselves and be the envy of those unhappy, maladjusted souls still searching to find themselves.

Fulfillment seems to mean endlessly developing, growing, expanding. It is often spoken of in the same breath as maturity. And maturing means ripening, filling out, coming to completion. Whether we speak of fulfillment or maturity, we get a sense of unrelenting forward and upward movement into the future.

Given our fascination with being fulfilled, it's no wonder that transitional experiences in which we feel empty, depleted, lost, or depressed are going to be interpreted as fulfillment's enemies. At best we see these times as potholes, detours on the path to fulfillment. At worst, they are signs we're reaching a dead end, an impasse.

Yet we continually undergo transitions. Often these are difficult times no matter how well prepared we are for them. Transitions are chaotic times during which we think we are going crazy. Feelings, fantasies, desires, fears, moods, and anxieties surface that we either never knew we had or thought we had already dealt with years ago. Then we may react with dismay, remorse, guilt, shame, worry, or more anxiety, partly because we can't make sense out of what is happening and partly because our understanding of maturing doesn't allow for such erratic and nonproductive behavior.

We do a disservice to ourselves and to others when we insist on a vision or interpretation of maturity that doesn't make allowances for these times of transition. St. Paul speaks about putting away childish things now that we are full grown. Many people interpret Paul as meaning that maturing is a linear, one-directional, evolutionary process where "progress is our most important product." But the reality of maturing is quite different. We move forward and backwards. We progress and we regress. We gain control and lose control. We may eventually discover that even our moving backwards is done in the service of moving forward. Like the pole vaulter we occasionally need to lean backwards in order to spring forward.

Today's society leads us to believe that maturing means getting more and more put together, more whole, more integrated. But there is another way of looking at maturity. What matures, ripens. But what ripens also reaches a point of rotting and disintegration. Can we accept the rotting as an integral dimension of our own maturing?

In these pages we are embarking on a journey of discovery. We will explore features common to all transitions; why people feel uneasy in transitions; why these feelings are so appropriate. By gaining a new appreciation of transitions, we can be enriched by them and navigate them more successfully.

And just as we focus on the details of unfamiliar scenery through a binocular's lenses, we shall be focusing on the unfamiliar terrain of transitions through the lenses of psychology, spirituality, and anthropology. Through the lens of psychology we'll see how transitions contribute to our growth and development. Spirituality will reveal how transitions offer the opportunity of connecting us to ultimate reality. Finally through the lens of anthropology—particularly through studies on the rites of passage—we can gain insight into transitions as transformative experiences in which we periodically die and are reborn during the life cycle.

Without these lenses we are left to our own devices to make sense of our experiences. And depending on how we interpret our transitions we can either create unnecessary problems or discover new possibilities. The interpretation makes all the difference in the world!

This book is divided into two parts. The first part draws on insights from psychology and rites of passage to focus on the threefold phases of a transition. The second part looks at transitions through the spiritual lens and considers the kind of attitude we need to negotiate transitions.

It is my hope that these chapters can teach us how to help not only ourselves but one another. And this we do not primarily through advice giving but by offering an understanding presence, letting others know that transitional experiences are angels of annunciation, not harbingers of despair.[1]

Part One

The Journey Is in the Breaks

We had the experience but missed the meaning.
(Attributed to T. S. Eliot)

How often have we listened to an anxious relative, friend, or even stranger tell us, "I don't know what's happening to me. I'm going through something, but I can't put my finger on what it is. Sometimes I think I'm losing my mind. Do you think that there's something wrong with me?"
Or how often have we told others, "I simply can't find the words to describe whatever it is that's taking place in my life. It's as if my world were falling apart."

"I don't know what's happening...I think I'm losing my mind...I can't find the words." Transitions are often difficult, but what makes them more difficult and even terrifying is being unable to find the words that make sense of them to ourselves or to others.

Consider the following transitions:

Puzzled parents trying to cope with a moody teenage boy whom a year earlier they proudly referred to as their little man. Now he seems determined to be doubly nasty towards them.

Brokenhearted over his girlfriend's decision to end their relationship, a young man feels lonelier than he's ever felt before.

A wife who has relied on her husband's advice for everything and is beginning to resent him even as she continues seeking his advice. She doesn't understand why she is becoming hostile towards the person whose advice she has always valued.

A husband who can no longer say whether he does or doesn't love his wife and wonders if they have any future together.

A deeply religious person who had always felt on intimate terms with God as friend and father has gradually become more aware of God's absence in her life. Now she wonders if she's losing her faith. Even worse, she sometimes thinks the whole idea of God is an illusion.

Formerly certain of his beliefs, a fifty-year-old man is now uncertain of everything he believes. His world is turned upside down.

A recent retiree who had been a workaholic in the office feels lost as he walks aimlessly around the house and offers his wife unsolicited advice on managing her affairs. Both of them are worried what life together means now.

A recently widowed man who feels anger towards his wife for having left him, guilt because he thinks he didn't do enough for her while she was alive, and relief that she has died because she is no longer suffering from a crippling illness. His mixed emotions baffle him.

The changes in the lives of these persons raise the question, What words can help us identify what is happening in our transitions? The question is important because words are an invaluable means of making sense out of our experiences. And if we cannot find meaning in the experience, of what value is the experience?

Fortunately, there is at our disposal a very ordinary word that appears in a variety of expressions to describe the richly complex experience we call a transition. *Break* is a remarkably rich word capable of describing different dimensions in transitions. Break. Breaking up, breaking down, breaking through, breaking point, the breaks, breaking away, breaking apart, breaking off, breaking out, breaking with, breaking in, breaking into, groundbreaking, taking a break, breaking even.

From among these many expressions, "breaking up," "breaking down," and "breaking through" best describe the three phases of a transition.

Three Movements in a Transition
Breaking Up

Breaking up is the first phase of change. It signifies an interruption in the way our lives are organized. The breakup could be as specific as divorce, retirement, or the death of a spouse. It could also be more encompassing. "Life holds no meaning for me and I don't know why," we might say as our world no longer seems to cohere or make sense. Breakups are often accompanied by tension, distress, hard feelings, and anxiety. When we are broken up we are distraught, upset, lonely, in pieces. The anticipation of breaking up is itself so painful that we often avoid it at any cost. We generally think of breaking up as a failure to mature rather than as the beginning of a process integral to our growth.

Related to breaking up is breaking away. It suggests going out on our own, finding our own way after having been part of or related to a larger unit or whole (e.g., the family, the company, or a religious organization). Breaking away might involve some sort of identity crisis since the larger unit has been the source of our identity. And implicit in our crisis is some form of internal breaking apart or fragmentation

"I'm not myself anymore. I'm being torn in different directions." Breaking apart is especially frightening if we have exercised a high degree of control over life. On the other hand, breaking apart might also be quite appealing if being controlling made us increasingly unhappy.

Breaking up also manifests itself in breaking with or breaking from the past. The traditions, customs, conventions in which we had been embedded and nurtured are frequently jettisoned or called into question as they begin to feel burdensome, oppressive, and alienating. Breaking up or away might appear sudden, from out of nowhere. But it is preceded by certain pressures to break out of confining boundaries, inhibitions, regulations. Developmentally we experience the need to break out of previously satisfying circumstances as growing pains.

But breaking out is also a way of speaking about the "symptoms" that signify the need to breakout, (e.g., anxiety, depression, anger). Just as we break out in cold sweats, a rash, or other physiological symptoms of some illness, so too we can break out in psychological symptoms of a condition that is dis-easing. Breaking out is the consequence of reaching the breaking point, the point beyond which we can no longer be self-restrained or contained in the status quo.

Breaking Down

The second cluster of expressions are connected with the second phase of change: *the breakdown*. Changes initiated in breaking up frequently lead to a breakdown. When we break down we often feel paralyzed, incompetent, depressed. Simple decisions are difficult to make. We feel lost and adrift. Breaking down suggests falling apart and losing composure in crying jags, laughing fits, or other irrational behaviors. When we are broken down we feel ready for the junk heap. We wonder where we have gone wrong, what we did that we ought not to have done or didn't do that we ought to have done.

Analyzing the reasons for what has happened to us is itself another way of understanding a breakdown. We speak of the need for an accounting, "Give me a breakdown!" Analysis, formal or informal, in a transition is often a critical self-inventory that people make when they are going through a divorce or a midlife crisis. "Did I fail? Where did I fail? What is wrong with me? How did it happen?" In breaking down or accounting for our behavior, we raise a host of questions.

This all takes place because we feel broke, spiritually, emotionally, physically. To be broken in this sense involves a leveling or dismantling of whatever has made us feel important or successful both in the interpersonal and professional dimensions of life. Self-esteem is often at an all-time low. And while this can be the cause for despair, it might also be an essential precondition for a change, as people in Alcoholics Anonymous can attest.

The breakdown occurs in the break, the gap or pause, in a person's life. While many of us would just as soon get on with our lives as get caught in this opening or break where we confront our brokenness, the break is necessary. Indeed, it is in the break that we might get the break we need. "Give me a break" or "I need a break" is a way of speaking about the need for an opportunity, a chance for a new direction. The breaks in which we might get breaks may last a day, a week, a year, or possibly several years. And only when we get a break can we achieve a breakthrough.

Breaking Through

Breaking through is the third phase of change. It is the insight or the vision that enables us to overcome the seemingly insurmountable obstacles of the breakdown. To get a break is to be given the opportunity to move beyond the impasse, to penetrate the darkness that has been so all-encompassing in the breakdown. It is a time of breaking in, of new light, vision, or life. But it also refers to a process of initiation. We break into new professions, work situations, and relationships. As novices we need to be broken in and guided as we forge a new identity and are assisted in developing this identity by tutors, mentors, spiritual directors. "Breaking through" also involves breaking into, in the sense of a release, a rebirth, a culmination. "They broke into songs of joy" conveys something of this breaking into.

"Breaking through" doesn't appear to be as negative as "breaking up" and "breaking down." When we think of a breakthrough, we think of a new perspective or fresh possibilities. But we break through by overcoming obstacles, resistances, and hurdles, sometimes at considerable expense. Think of labor pains or the strenuous efforts required to run a marathon!

It is important to point out that there is considerable overlapping in breaking up, down, and through. Much of what we achieve by breaking up takes place as a result of some breakthrough, while the latter might lead to an eventual break or breakdown. Breakups, breakdowns, and breakthroughs do not proceed in an orderly A-B-C fashion, nor is there any neat separation of one from the others. Yet each is essential in a complete experience of transition.

Rites of Passage

Ordinarily we don't think of the times of breaking up, down, and through as indicative of any momentous transformations in life unless, that is, we view them through the lens of a contemporary rite of passage.

Rites of passage? Why talk about primitive rituals performed either before any of us were born or in remote places we have never heard of? What could a tribe of unsophisticated illiterates have to offer us? For one thing these "illiterates" recognized that during the life cycle there are times to die and times to be reborn, times for saying good-bye to the past and hello to the future. They realized what we so frequently lose sight of, namely, we can't cling forever to identities built up through roles, status, achievements, and possessions, especially if these prevent us from striking out in new directions.

Realizing these things, they knew how important it was that their members be properly informed and prepared for these moments of transformation. Celebrating these passages was also a way for all the tribal members to say to those going through the rites, "We're with you. We support you. You're not alone." Although they were primitives, they certainly were more knowledgeable than we in realizing the importance of communal support for those going through the ordeals of transition.

The late anthropologist Victor Turner spent much of his career studying these rites among African tribes, and we can summarize some of his important findings. There were three phases in the rites: the preliminal, or phase of separation; the liminal, or in-between phase; the postliminal, or time of reincorporation. We might think of breaking up, down, and through as roughly corresponding with the ritual of transformation in which the novices separated themselves from their tribe, entered into an in-between zone, and then were reincorporated into society.

In the first phase those about to go through this period of transformation separated themselves from the rest of the tribe and entered a special place in the woods or forest where the ritual was to be conducted. Separating themselves from their familiar world for the unknown might have been scary business, since those who had already been initiated never disclosed to the uninitiated what happened in these rituals.

The secrecy surrounding these ceremonies underscored the importance their community attributed to the rites.

Arriving at the place where the ritual was to occur, these "novices," or beginners, entered what Turner described as "liminal" space and time. The word *liminal* comes from the latin *limen,* which means "threshold." When we stand between two rooms and are neither in one nor the other, we are on the threshold. If someone were to ask, "Where are you?" technically we would have to say, "Neither here nor there—not in this room nor the other." In the liminal phase of the ritual, the novices could no longer be identified as the persons they had been in their society nor the persons they would become. They were somewhere in between—in a neutral zone or no-man's-land—waiting for a new identity. And that is where they had to be. They had died to their previous mode of living, but they had not yet been born to a new mode.

The liminal phase is worthy of our consideration since it might help us understand why we need to go through our own in-between times when we're not sure who we are or what is to become of us. It's frightening not to have any idea what direction we are heading. The difference between those who went through the passage rituals and ourselves is that we do not think of our own liminal time as the necessary break to prepare ourselves for new beginnings.

Finally the novices entered the postliminal phase. The period of transformation was completed, and they were ready to assume new responsibilities as adult members of the tribe. They knew what was expected of them. Since everyone acknowledged that these novices had achieved a new status, they were ready to resume their places in their tribe. Unfortunately, since many of us are uncertain we are going through major changes or are unable to identify the nature of these changes or are going through them alone, it is very difficult to negotiate these transitions without others' help.

In the chapters that follow, if we look at periods of breaking up, down, and through against the background of rites of passage, we can recognize that while our experiences on one level are "secular," on another they are periods of spiritual transformation or rebirth. Of course, we don't ordinarily refer to these times of breaking as times of rebirth. But whether we are speaking of seeing things in a new light or from a different perspective, we are speaking about something akin to a rite of passage, a spiritual transformation.

In addition to drawing on rites of passage to assist us in understanding our transitions, we shall also be enlisting the help of psychologists. When we go through our transitions, we undergo momentous changes on the intrapersonal and interpersonal levels. Previous ways of relating to spouse, children, parents, or the like no longer seem to work, and new ways haven't emerged. Lacking insight into what is happening, we find ourselves in the dark about what to do or say as changes occur. We can be greatly helped in our struggle to make sense out of these changes by consulting people who are especially knowledgeable about personality development and how this development affects our breaking up, down, and through.

Chapter 1

Breaking Up

> Any real change implies the breakup of the world as one has always known it, the loss of all that gave one identity, the end of safety. And at such a moment, unable to see and not daring to imagine what the future will now bring forth, one clings to what one knew, or thought one knew; to what one possessed or dreamed that one possessed. Yet it is only when man is able, without bitterness or self-pity, to surrender a dream he has long cherished, or a privilege he has long possessed, that he is set free—that he has set himself free—for higher dreams, for greater privileges.
>
> *James Baldwin, Nobody Knows My Name* [1]

Primitive tribal rites of passage are preceded by clear-cut rites of separation in which those who are to go through the rites are separated from the ordinary day-to-day existence of tribal life in order to go through the spiritual rebirth that the rites afford. Clearly, the candidates understand the significance of breaking away from the space-time dimension of the tribe for the re-creative space and time of the rites. Whatever their fears or anxieties might be as they leave the known for the unknown, the goal of spiritual rebirth is worth the risk.

Unfortunately, today when we go through the period of breaking up or separating from the status quo as the preliminary step to our own transformation through a transition, we have no idea that we too might be undergoing a spiritual and psychological rebirth. Ordinarily there are no gurus, no tribal elders or spiritual directors available to help interpret and guide us on our journey.

In this chapter we'll consider contemporary experiences of separating or breaking up. The questions addressed in this chapter are, How do people describe their experiences of breaking up? From whom or what do people break away? Is it necessary to go through periods of change in which breaking up figures so prominently? Addressing these questions not only illumines our own experiences but also clarifies why what we are going through is essential if our breaking away is to lead to any real transformation.

Developmental Transitions

Throughout our lives we attempt to satisfy two basic longings. They are the longing to be a separate, distinct person and the longing to belong, to connect with and be part of a larger whole. This means that sometimes we need to discover who we are apart from others and at other times we need to be in relation to others. (Actually both needs are always present, but one need is usually in the foreground while the other is in the background.) "Apart from" means differentiating me from what is not me—discovering me and mine and separating them from you and yours—redrawing the boundaries between myself and the other. "In relation to" refers to connecting with, being intimately involved or part of a larger whole, integrating. It means being available to others in a way I could not have been when I was identified with them. The process of differentiating who we are apart from and in relation to others takes place throughout the life cycle in developmental transitions. Through these transitions we come to a more distinct sense of who we are as well as what is other than or different from us.

In looking at some of these developmental changes in the adult life cycle, we shall draw on insights of Robert Kegan, a constructive developmental psychologist who chairs the Institute for the Management of Lifelong Education at Harvard.

I Am Not What I Was

Developmental changes in the adult life cycle occur when our way of knowing and feeling about the world undergoes a profound change. The change involves the breaking up or death of one world and the birth of another in relation to self and others. It implies losing ourselves and others in one way and finding them in a new way. Transitions generate a tension between a side of the self that needs to break with the status quo and a side that feels obligated to defend it because it is still identified with it. This tension is best described in the statement, "I am not what I was but I am not *not* what I was either."

"I am not what I was." When we go through transitions, we often say, "I'm not my old self anymore," or "I can't go back to being the me I was," or "I'm not the old me anymore! I used to be so agreeable. People called me Mr. Nice Guy—always saying yes—a real soft touch!" We are looking back on an "old" self or a self which in some way we have outgrown. And we are looking at it from the perspective of a newly emerging self. From this vantage point we feel angry or disdainful towards that old self. Something new is breaking out.

"I am not *not* what I was either." Some of the statements about not being the old agreeable self can also refer to a side of ourselves that still holds. It still has a voice—a sadness that something *special* is dying. Or when we speak about not being ourselves anymore, if that implies the good old days, it is a side of the self, the old self, that is speaking on behalf of the stability we once had. So in the description, "I am not *not* what I was," the "not *not*" is a way of saying, "I *am* the me I was—the old self." Something of ourselves is still back there and is threatened with being lost. It is the me or side of the self from which we have not yet broken away.

If we put both parts of the statement together, we have "I am not what I was (i.e., a new self is emerging—being born) but I am not not what I was either (i.e., the old me has not moved over into the present and is hankering after the past). The purpose in using all these negatives—"not" and "not not" to describe the emerging new and the old self—is to suggest our not being fully in one place or the other, not at home with the old or with the new but somewhere in between.

In the preceding analysis, it is evident that there are possibilities for real conflict as we begin breaking away from a previous way of identifying ourselves. "I'm not the me I was" can be in conflict with "I'm not not the me I was." This conflict is a felt tension, not necessarily the result of any reflective analysis.

From the Socializing Self to the Self-authorizing Self

The tension between a side of the self that is emerging and a side that has been around for a while exists in all the different transitions throughout the life cycle. How it is played out concretely depends in large measure on the specific kind of transition in the life cycle we are going through. For example, consider the kind of transition many of us are experiencing today in the family, in church communities, in society— the transition from relying almost exclusively on others to relying on ourselves to determine how to think and feel. The new self that is emerging is fresh, fragile, unsure of itself.

Being unsteady, it might feel fearful of being reabsorbed or sucked back into being the compliant, dependent personality it now rejects as utterly confining and smothering. Still the old self—the side that has gotten its strokes the only way it knew how, through pleasing others and being validated by others' approval—is shaken up by the new self's attitude. The old self accuses this upstart of being out for itself and cold, selfish, or indifferent towards its past agreeable way of relating to others.

The emerging new self speaks, "I don't want anything to do with people making claims on me. I've had it with people whose opinions and feelings and ideas I've had to put up with all these years. Making it seem like they were mine! Let me run my own life!" And the old me answers, "You're just out for yourself, aren't you? That's all you care about, not other people's feelings. Just what *you* want! What's wrong with you?"

What's obvious is that the new me, struggling to assert itself, has had it with others who it feels have held it in bondage. But what isn't so obvious is whether it has also had it with the old me that had comfortably sided with the others, the oppressors.

In other words, in the beginning of many developmental transitions, we shall be angry not only with people from whom we are trying to differentiate ourselves (parents, peers, a spouse) but also with a side of ourselves, the old self, that at the time seemed to love singing others' songs. To an observer it might seem that we are simply saying no to people who made up our past. The truth is we are equally saying no to the side of ourselves that was part of that past.

But this being at odds with ourselves can also be seen in earlier life transitions. During the terrible twos, the protest against mom and dad is as much a protest against the baby's old self that was part of mom and dad. "I'm not you and I'm not the me I was." Similarly, the adolescent protest is not simply a protest of "I'm not you" but also "I'm not the old me. When I put you down, I am putting down the old cuddly me." Of course, adolescents don't express the protest in these words. No, they just grow ugly. They say nasty things to get their folks upset. They smell nasty to get everybody upset. And they emit gross body sounds at the kitchen table. That's enough to get people to forget the cute, cuddly thing of late childhood! People in all developmental transitions get very oppositional. The newly emerging self seemingly has to react with some violence if it is to survive. The new me is like a young David struggling with an old, dying Goliath that has been around for a while and doesn't easily yield the turf.

The opening lines in the parable of the prodigal son (Luke 15:11) can also be interpreted as the beginning of a transition in which the younger son opposed himself to his father. His demand, "Father, let me have the share of the estate that would come to me," is chilling when we realize that he would not have received his inheritance until his father died. In effect he was telling his father to drop dead! However, his defiance is directed not only towards his father but towards the side of himself that would have preferred remaining comfortably at home. And when he leaves home, it isn't only his father who loses him: he loses himself as he had known himself. His journey is as much a process of discovering himself in a new way as it is of discovering his father.

A dramatic example of an oppositional stance was given by a sixty-year-old man as he recounted an incident that happened when he was eleven years old.

> Funny how things happen that change your whole life. I remember the first time I ever felt fear, sudden terror without conscious reason. I was eleven years old. We were in the kitchen. My father came in. He said, "Well, Mother..."—the rest I can't remember, because a blind fear came over me. *I was afraid of*

my mother. I loved my mother. She was the one we all relied on. My father always spoke of her good judgment. "A wonderful woman, your mother. Take her advice and you won't go wrong." That was what we all did. She made the decisions for all the family and they always seemed right. We often talked of her plans for my future. They seemed right too. I *couldn't* be afraid of her, but I *was.* Why? Everything in me was rigid, on guard, watching...asking, Why? Our old dog stood there wagging his tail—like my father, tame. My mother asked my father to do something. He went out again. I looked at her. I *hated* her. I knew I had to get away from her. How? An answer rushed up in me. "Disobey her—right now." That was what I feared—defying her: that was what I had to do. After a little, she told me to do something. I have no idea now what it was; it might have been something I wanted to do; but I *had* to disobey. I remember the feeling, as though I were pulling everything inside myself into a tight ball; and "something" inside myself said, "This is it." I refused obedience. She commanded; again I refused. I wouldn't answer any question. I hung onto my refusal. If I argued, I might get weak; she might win. Then she threatened; I refused. And then she cried. I had never seen her cry before. I felt the ball unwinding. I mustn't. I went out of the kitchen into the sunlight that had lost all its brightness. I sat down in the shelter of the woodpile back of the barn. I can still remember how strangely unfamiliar the sticks of wood looked. This was a world I had never seen before. I felt absolutely and completely alone, faced with the terrible responsibility of myself and of what I had chosen. I could never go back.

Then, after what seemed an eternity of time, my mother called and I went in to supper. Everything was the same, yet everything was different. Neither my mother nor I spoke of what had happened. But it had happened. I felt alone—and often I was afraid. I didn't know enough to choose, but I knew I had made an irrevocable choice which meant I had to decide for myself—even when I was uncertain. I had to find out by myself, for myself.[2]

We can understand how confusing and tiring it is to experience the tug between the old me that is intimidated by the change that's in the air and the new me fearful that nothing will change. Back and forth! Back and forth! Maybe we can also understand why people who are going through this kind of a struggle in a transition might get depressed. Depression is about loss. And in this tug of war between the not me and the not not me, as the new me is emerging the old is dying. Our way of knowing ourselves is changing, and the change involves loss. What is at stake is the very way in which we relate to ourselves and our world. Later we shall see that being depressed might be exactly the appropriate response to the experience of loss in transitional changes.

For many of us the transition from relying on others to relying on ourselves means being torn between the old me, identified with its loyalties and affiliations, and the emerging new me, questioning those same loyalties. Among these loyalties can be family, friends, church authorities, a certain understanding of who God is and what God wants, or many others. Alternately, we can feel guilty for being disloyal and defiant towards these loyalties. We can also feel sad for the dying self as we have known it, self that had made us feel special. There's no way around it.

Robert Kegan studied the kind of developmental

change we have been describing. He often writes of the transition from relying on others to relying on oneself in determining how to think and feel. The inability to assess one's worth or value independently of others, a stage of development usually achieved in late adolescence, he calls the "socializing mind."[3] People in this stage see themselves mirrored through the approving or disapproving eyes of others. Seeing themselves apart from others, that is, defining themselves in their own eyes, is not possible at this stage. They do not really experience themselves as having a perspective on themselves independent of how others see them. They really do not experience themselves as having separate selves.

If Kegan is correct, then many in our society, with its civic and religious institutions, have not gotten beyond the stage of the socializing mind. This is especially true of women, who have traditionally been defined (and so defined themselves) as givers and nurturers for others. As a result, any consideration they might have given to defining themselves in terms of their own goals often had the effect of making them feel that they were selfish, only thinking of themselves. And often when women married, they set aside their own legitimate aspirations and ambitions in favor of their husband's. Those defined by others do not have their own voice—which is a metaphor for saying that they do not have a separate self and they remain silent. Some see this as the cause of higher rates of depression among women than men. However, it is important not to forget that the socializing mind is initially an *achievement* of late adolescence. It's crucial at some point to be able to take into account the expectations and concerns of others in putting together and interpreting one's world. The problem emerges when individuals and groups of people can't get *beyond* looking to others' expectations about how to live life. Such people don't get bigger psychologically. They become "grown-ups," not people continuing to grow up. What was an achievement becomes a liability.

Being overheld or stalled at this stage can make us feel guilty or disloyal. Why? Calling into question others' judgments feels like an act of disloyalty not only to others but to the side of ourselves that still needs others' approval. About this state of affairs Kegan says, "An infallible guide outside ourselves, in which we comfortably invest authority and to which authority we pledge loyalty, fidelity, and faith—this is the essence of psychological dependence."[4]

Scripting

The transition of breaking away from the old me (dependent on other people writing my life script) to the new me (a separate, distinct self) involves two things: recognizing the people "out there" who write my script, and recognizing and confronting the people "inside" of me dictating how I am to live my life. It is crucial that we identify these inner voices or authorities in order to complete the process of differentiating the self from others. The inner voices or scripts can so powerfully govern behavior that they might be described as a kind of possession, script possession.

Scripts are lines, bits of dialogue that, strung together, give a story—not our own, of course, but someone else's. We then act out these scripts. Many of these scripts were written for us very early in life, but some are also being written as we mature and get older. What is particularly disturbing about the scripts is that we have been led to believe we authored them. Lines like "I'm no good" and "I'll never amount to much" float around in our brains, and we say to ourselves, "That's me; that's what I think." But it isn't me. It's them, disguised as me, telling myself it's me.

Scripting is the ghosts of parents, teachers, relatives, the church, and culture, identifying who we are, whether we're good or bad, how we should live our lives. Can this scripting be exorcised? Yes, but it takes time. The exorcism begins by differentiating their voices from our own. Whose voice is it that says, "I'm no good?" What's its origin? Perhaps a parent scolding us, "You're no good"—no matter what we did to please. Who says in us, "I can't do anything right?" The voices of well-intentioned people who assume our responsibilities because they thought us incompetent? Do they live on in us? Or do the voices represent stereotypical attitudes coming from our culture? How many of these voices roam about needing to be exorcised? Whose voices are these? Ours or theirs? Answering these questions is essential to the exorcism.

Along with this task comes another: determining what we really think or feel or want to do. Not an easy determination since we deny "they" have been telling us what to think, feel, and do. All along *we* thought *we* were thinking, feeling, and doing. Can we listen to our own resistances, urges, and inclinations as we differentiate our voice from the others'? For in the resistance, urge, and inclination we may find the clue to what we really think or feel or desire.

These urges, feelings, resistances that attend our breaking up seem frightening because they are so contrary to the way we present or see ourselves. Yet they are important sources of self-knowledge precisely because they seem so unlike us. The paradox is that the inner voices we have assumed to be ours are not, while the troublesome feelings and thoughts we had considered alien are actually us. Identifying the source of these alien responses is as important a task as identifying our inner voices. Shortly we shall have occasion to reflect on the unconscious source of these feelings and thoughts and the potential they offer for a more comprehensive understanding of who we are.

This whole process is a transition from the socializing mind, in which we are governed by others' expectations, to a self that Kegan has called the "self-authorizing mind." We write our own scripts and are the authors of our lives. The self-authorizing mind is a mind capable of naming its own standards, its own norms, its own ideology. By this Kegan means a person no longer defined by others and their expectations but self-defining. The transition can take years and involves the breaking apart of one world and the breakthrough of another.

As in the struggle between the old and the new, in our transitions we can expect to experience contradictory feelings. From the perspective of the old self that we are leaving behind (i.e., the self defined by relationships), we might feel we are being cold, distant, uncaring, and out for ourselves as we break away from seeing ourselves in others' eyes. But from the perspective of the newly emerging self we might be fearful of once more losing ourselves in the relationships that had defined us. These claims and counterclaims issuing from both the old and the new self are all the more distressing because of the absence of any ritualized way of acknowledging the death of the old and the birth of the new self. It is especially this death and rebirth that were duly acknowledged and celebrated by tribal elders in rites of passage. Within a limited time span the struggle towards transformation took place. Once it had occurred, there was no way in which those who had gone through the passage rites could return to their former identity.

From the Self-Authorizing Self to the Interindividual Self

Becoming self-authorizing, or capable of naming our own standards and thus determining for ourselves the basis for governing life, is a considerable step beyond being governed by others' expectations. We are able to take charge of our own lives. The balance at which we have arrived, however, might not be permanent. Many people settle in here and look out on the world through the lens of their own new standards, evaluating others' truths, ideologies, and standards. But others move beyond this balance into another transition. And this transition is every bit as upsetting as the previous one.

In this transition we begin to experience as relative the standards, norms, and ideological base by which we have governed ourselves and through which we have ordered our world. In other words we are becoming painfully aware that our truth or the truth of the group through which we have ordered our world is not the *only* truth. There are other truths, other standards, other moral norms for determining what is true and what is false, what is right and what is wrong. As we are breaking away from understanding our truth not as *the* truth but as *a* truth, we might feel as if the world were coming to an end.

"You mean...Jesus might not be the only savior for everybody! You mean there might be some truth in Buddhism. You mean we might be able to learn something from people who don't see things the way we do!" The new me sees that its old way of understanding had been too isolating, too narrow and controlling. But the old me is indignant over what's happening and sends a message to the new me that it is out of control, weak, evil, morally corrupt, a libertine—throwing out standards that have governed the person's outlook and conduct for years. And sure enough! The new me, being new, an upstart, feels alternately freed up—no boundaries—and downright wicked! And in its struggles to free itself from the old self's insistence on conformity to the one and only truth, the new self's initial reaction is what we would expect: protest.

"There isn't any truth; one is as good as the other." Then all hell breaks loose as we feel that we might be standing on the quicksand of moral relativism. Indeed, during this kind of transition, we question the meaning of everything. We wonder whether we are believers or atheists. Does anything add up? The disappearance of meaning takes place, and the old me says "You fool! See what you've done! Don't you wish things were safe and simple like they were before? I bet being a Moonie or a fundamentalist doesn't sound so bad now, does it? They're singing songs, clapping hands, praising the Lord and all you can do is cry out, 'Oh God! Where are you?' So are you happy?" Although many transitions are characterized by disillusionment, this transition in which our truth is relativized is especially disillusioning.

The transition from regarding our truth as normative (in deciding others' claims to truth) is a transition from the self-authorizing mind or self to what Kegan calls the *interindividual* self or its equivalent, the interdependent self.[4] Going through this transition, we become aware that the truth that is normative for us is not *the* truth. We are open to the possibility that the perspective others have on the truth not only has validity but is capable of enriching our own perspective. The claim "I have the truth" gives way to a more modest claim that "we each have ways of understanding the truth and can each be enriched by one another's approach to the truth."

Persona Identity Transitions

There is yet another set of experiences in which breaking away occurs. These experiences sometimes overlap developmental shifts or changes. At other times they do not. For example, if a woman separates from her husband, she might be going through a shift from the socializing mind to the self-authorizing mind described by Kegan. But she may also be breaking away from her identity as a wife of her husband. The two kinds of change can take place independently of one another, or they might be interrelated. But they are not the same. A woman whose husband is supportive of the developmental shift might not feel the necessity of physically separating from her husband or divorcing him. On the other hand, she might divorce him and not necessarily be going through a developmental change. Consider, too, a man whose wife has died. Whether he goes through any developmental shift, he still needs to go through the transition of becoming single again. So while the experiences described in this section might occur along with developmental changes, they need not. And I think they are best described as *persona identity transitions* in which the person breaks away, or *disidentifies,* from what Carl Jung referred to as the persona. We can understand some of the transitional experiences of breaking away by interpreting them by way of Jung's contribution to an understanding of the persona and the shadow.

Persona

We have to adapt to our environments. Adapting means fitting in, accommodating, sometimes conforming to the environment. This is accomplished primarily through the persona, or mask. We present ourselves within our environment as a teacher, business person, minister, or whatever. We relate to others as husband, wife, mother, father, son, daughter, or friend. We expect to come across to others in certain ways. And we expect others in turn to have their expectations of how we are to act. So being a father means a man will project the way he wants to appear to his son, while at the same time doing justice to the expectations of his culture with its civil and religious institutions. Thus, the persona is a blend of personal and cultural expectations.

In this way a quasi identity is built up around the persona or personae we wear. If someone has been a dentist for twenty years, then that person's way of relating to others is frequently governed and sometimes dictated by the dentist's persona. In fact, the relationship between who we are and what we do is so intimate that right after introductions are made, we tell what we do and ask what the other does. Sharing our role or function (the persona) and knowing those of others free us up to talk because now we know where we stand relative to others. Of course, such an identity is a quasi identity. There is much more to us than any one mask we wear. The dentist is not just a dentist, nor a wife just a wife. Yet ten or twenty years of relating in and through a particular persona takes its toll. After so long a time, our way of expressing who we are is very limited. The persona might be the primary vehicle through which we have come to know ourselves or be known to others. Certain persons don't seem capable of relating to others except through a professional persona. Whether at the office or on social visits or at home, they can speak about nothing but their business. Having no outside interests or hobbies, their world of discourse is limited to what they know and do best— their work. Unfortunately, all we know about some people whom we have known for years is limited to their presence through the one persona.

One way of understanding what is happening when we go through persona identity transitions is to view ourselves as separating from a habitual way of relating to our world via one persona. In other words, when we find ourselves increasingly dissatisfied at home or at work, it's possible that our manner of adapting (our persona) no longer adequately expresses who and what we have become in the work or home environment. If, for example, a person in midlife finds a growing dissatisfaction in a job or if a man finds his way of relating to wife and children and himself increasingly difficult, what does this say about the fit between the reality of the person and the persona through which it is expressed?

When we say we no longer know who we are, we may be expressing an increasing tension or even a split between our old persona and a growing though vague new self-understanding. This way of describing the situation might lead us to view the personality as real (the inner reality, the person behind the mask) and the persona, the mask, as unreal. It is unfortunate that the very word *mask* suggests phoniness and unreality. On the one hand, Jung certainly never intended to imply that the persona is, in and of itself, phony or unreal or just a covering. Quite the contrary; at its best the persona discloses and channels a certain dimension of the personality. It can and does express something very real about us. On the other hand, no one persona can forever express our total reality. The personality rigidly confined to one mode of expression will feel as cramped as a size-twelve foot in a size-nine shoe!

Perhaps this explains why, in the process of breaking away from an inadequate persona, some of us feel phony about ourselves in our relationships with others. This feeling of being phony comes from our awareness that the old ways of relating no longer match our changing self-perceptions. It might be truer to say that in this first phase of a persona identity transition, we sense that we are not who we pretend to be; we resent being treated and referred to in terms of our old persona. "That's not me anymore but don't ask me who I am because I don't know," would be our response.

This painful disidentification from the old way of relating to no longer knowing how to relate authentically is the context within which it is possible to understand the crisis of commitment that many of us seem to encounter during such transitions. Those who have long-standing commitments to marriage, ministry, or career find they are unsure whether they are really committed to anyone or anything. A woman who has been married for twenty-five years wonders what is wrong with her. She had always thought she was committed to her husband, but now she isn't certain. Not that she is indifferent; she isn't. She simply can no longer say one way or the other where she is in their relationship.

Understanding that what is taking place in this area of her life is symptomatic of a larger, global breakup or disidentification taking place within every other area of her life is necessary so that she can make some sense of her experiences. Perhaps her ambiguous feelings can be attributed to the growing distance between her commitment and the habitual way through which she has expressed that commitment, that is, via the persona. The point is that it is the previous way of experiencing commitment that may be dying and not necessarily the commitment itself.

Me and My Shadow

Breaking away from a previous identity can occur simply because of a relational change: a divorce, the death of a spouse, or retirement. Circumstances render a person no longer a wife, mother, employee. Breaking away can also occur because of the limitations of any one persona to express adequately our total potential for development. Restricting our self-expression along certain narrow, predictable ways leads to a counterreaction from within: the call to break away from our limited and limiting self-presentation via the persona. Just as in a developmental transition we need to listen to our inner urges, feelings, and resistances that contradict the chorus of others' voices governing our lives (voices that we had thought to be our own but that derive from external sources), so too in persona identity transitions. Both the counterreaction to the limited persona and the inner resistances are often signs of what Jung referred to as the "shadow."

We can appreciate what Jung means by the shadow and its contribution to changing our self-understanding and the ways we might break away from our habitual way of relating to others by considering Jesus' words in Luke's gospel. "Why look at the speck in your brother's eye when you miss the plank in your own?" (6:41–42). What's this plank that we fail to see in our eye when we point out the speck in another's eye?

Suppose we work in a large office and every fifteen minutes we take a five-minute coffee break. Every time we go down the hall for our coffee, we see this other fellow standing there sipping his coffee. Shaking our head in disbelief, we return to our desk and tell the fellow next to us that we have seen the laziest guy in the world. "Every time I get coffee I see the same Bozo standing there! What a goldbricker! Good thing the boss doesn't see him there. I have a mind to tell him off!" Who in the office has the plank in his eye?

Or imagine there's a bloody accident on the highway. We decide we've got to stop and see what happened. We notice a large crowd of people who have gathered and are staring at the accident victim. We say to ourselves, "Gee, these people are something else! They're all staring at this guy covered in blood. Gawkers! That's what they are!" And we continue staring at the victim until the ambulance arrives. Who in the crowd has the plank in his eye?

Or think of some well-known televangelist who is forever chastising people for their sexual immorality. And then his name appears in the headlines for propositioning someone. Who's got the plank?

What is a plank? The plank is our shadow, a kind of alter ego we can't recognize as belonging to our own personality. It's the me in me of which I am simply unaware. For example, if we think we are about as liberal a Democrat as there is, there is a strong possibility a very conservative Republican is lurking in the background. Or if we think we are a believing Christian, there might be a little atheist lodged in our unconscious who doesn't buy all this Jesus stuff. Or if we're against capital punishment on one level, on another there's a me who would like nothing better than to strangle someone.

What happens when we can't recognize this plank or shadow in ourselves? Jung tells us that we *project* the shadow onto others. By this he means we see in others what we can't see in ourselves. You are the lazy person, not me. You are always taking the coffee break; I just happen to be there. You are the ghoulish voyeurs at the scene of an accident; I'm just concerned. You are the perverts who lust after X-rated movies. Not me! I want to see them (in their entirety, of course) so that I can censor them. And I demand to censor *all* of them! Parents sometimes get angry at their children and they don't know why until it dawns on them that what they have never liked about themselves is present to some degree in their children. Chips off the old blocks, or slivers off the big planks!

If we want to know who or what our plank or shadow is, all we need to do is think of one or two people whom we despise, people whose eyes we'd like to scratch out. Having thought about them, we can now ask ourselves what it is that we despise in them. Then we might glimpse the nature of the plank or shadow we carry within ourselves.

Although the shadow is always the unacknowledged side of ourselves that we see in projection, it doesn't always appear negatively in others. We might admire positive qualities in others that we think are nonexistent in ourselves. Someone who is always giving might admire a person who knows when to say no and draw the boundaries. Or someone who always feels the need to be in control might be drawn towards a free spirit.

We saw how script possession in developmental transitions might lead to feeling a certain inner pressure not to be compliant. In these persona identity transitions our shadow side might engender feelings of hostility towards being Mr.

Nice Guy and impel us to break away from this identity. These pressures initially might feel uncomfortable because they go contrary to our prevailing image of ourselves. While we might have admired others who knew when to say no, we had never owned the possibility that we could be so assertive. But gradually as we become aware of feelings and thoughts that counter our long-standing image of ourselves, it is possible that we can begin to integrate this more assertive side, which had been a dimension of our shadow. The payoff in paying attention to the shadow is that the breakup of a previous self-understanding via the conscious integration of the shadowy assertive side leads to greater awareness of self and others.

What is the function of the shadow? It is frightening to acknowledge certain traits we despise in others as being part of our own psychological makeup. It's as if Mahatma Gandhi discovered a bit of Hitler in himself—the side of himself that could be dictatorial. Yet every saint has a bit of the sinner even as every sinner has a bit of the saint. The shadow insulates us from this unpleasant reality.

But there is another function of the shadow, since even what can contribute to a richer personality can appear threatening. It can seem so alien to a current self-understanding. Who or what would we be like if we owned what we see in projected form in others, whether positive or negative? Certainly it would mean losing one way of being ourselves without knowing how or whether we would be at all.

Besides recognizing that we project what we don't like about ourselves onto others, what can we do with this unknown shadow side? We need to *befriend* our shadow. Befriending the shadow means being both courageous and compassionate. It takes courage to admit that we are not all light and good, that what we despise in others we may possess to a degree in ourselves. What we hate in a serial killer we may potentially bear within ourselves. And being courageous might also mean acknowledging and being willing to develop within ourselves those qualities we had admired and praised in others...at a safe distance from ourselves. Why? Because developing our gifts is risky business. We do not know how it will change our lives or how others will react to these changes, especially if the change affects people close to us.

Befriending the shadow also requires compassion towards what we regard as ugly in ourselves as well as in others. Just as we would tend any wound, we need to tend what is weird or strange in ourselves. Compassionate engagement with this unknown side might lead to a partnership with dimensions of ourselves we had ignored for half a lifetime.

The transitional experiences we have considered indicate two ways in which we break up or break away. We have seen that as we go through developmental transitions, we are breaking from patterns of relating that are unique to various stages of development. Breaking up in these instances signifies momentous change occurring over a long period in which one world is dying and another is being born. The tension in our lives is between a side of the self favoring the status quo and a side favoring change.

But we have also seen that major changes that occur in persona identity transitions can be attributed to a growing dissatisfaction with a quasi identity established over a number of years. Increasingly we feel a tension between our self-presentation (persona) and the reality that we are, a reality that is inadequately being expressed through this persona. In our breaking away from what had given us an identity, we no longer resemble our former selves. We are broken up. Can we come together again in a new way? Is there reason for hope or despair? Much depends on what transpires during this time of being broken down. There is both danger and opportunity in the middle phase of a transition, the phase to which we next direct our attention.

Chapter 2

Breaking Down:
Setups and Letdowns

> From a psychological perspective liminal space is
> initially deconstructive. It dissolves our previous
> expectations as to ways of experiencing ourselves
> and our relationship to the world. Then it offers us
> a new vision of ourselves and our relationships.
> We are regenerated, recreated almost from the
> bottom up, as new, more fully integrated and
> mature people.
>
> Robert Moore, *The Magician Within*[1]

Essential to understanding liminality is its in-betwee-
ness. It points to the fact that those undergoing tribal
rites of passage as well as those in transition experience an
ambiguous status. In rites of passage, since the novices
undergo a transformation from one state of being to
another, they are both dying and being reborn. Symbolically, this is represented by huts and tunnels that are at
once tombs and wombs; by snake symbolism (for the
snake appears to die but only sheds its skin and appears in
a new one); by nakedness (which is at once the mark of a
newborn infant and of a corpse prepared for burial). Turner
notes that processes of undoing, dissolution, and decom-
position are accompanied by processes of growth and
transformation.[2]

This ambiguous status also means that the novices no longer fit into the clearly defined categories of the society from which they came. Being unclassifiable, they are "ritually" unclean—out of place, in the margins. But not fitting in anywhere is itself necessary for spiritual rebirth. Because of their status they are secluded, hidden from the ordinary commerce of tribal life. Since these novices cannot be clearly defined, the tribal community also sees them as having a close connection with superhuman power or deity—the unbounded, the infinite, the limitless. And it is within this context of the sacred space and time of liminality that the novices experience rebirth.

Today, as we go through the liminal phase of a transition, we might feel broken down. We don't know what is happening to us. On the one hand, we might speak of ourselves as feeling run down, falling apart, at our wits end, crazy. We might cry that we do not feel anything anymore. It's as if we were dead. We read the obituary columns with greater attention. On the other hand, even as we speak about feeling dead, we also seem to be in touch with feelings we had never noticed, interests newly discovered or long neglected, and emerging sensitivities towards family, friends and coworkers.

While we might have had a clear idea of our place in society, we no longer do (e.g., if we were married and are now widowed or divorced,) and we now feel abandoned by friends as if we were unclean. Or even if no one has abandoned us, we still might feel isolated from those with whom we had been intimate. Physical proximity of family and friends doesn't insure freedom from feelings of isolation. We can be lonely with or without others present. And sometimes observing how others enjoy intimacies with friends or lovers simply highlights our own loneliness or inability to connect.

If God's presence had previously been a felt presence of consolation, now we may feel God's presence as absence. Whether by "God" we mean a greater power, Being, Buddha,

Jesus, or Meaning, this God is nowhere to be found. God is a nowhere God for many who experience this uninvited break or rupture in their lives.

While our experiences of breaking down resemble the liminal phase or in-between time in rites of passage, there is one important difference. There aren't many elders or spiritual mentors to help us understand that our confusion, our experiences of falling apart, our newly emerging feelings, our preoccupation with our own mortality, our frightening experience of this God who is "beyond" any previous experiences of God, that all this belongs to the experience of death and rebirth in our own rites of passage. There is no one to tell us, when we feel we no longer fit the categories in which we have seen ourselves or have been seen by others, that this too belongs to the tranformative process.

This confusion about ourselves and our world will become apparent as we explore contemporary liminality— the break or opening—in which people repeatedly describe feeling disillusioned and depressed. In this and the following chapter we shall explore the potentials for growth in and through our experiences of disillusionment and depression that accompany transitions.

Disillusionment is the wake-up call to the fact that we feel we have been "set up" in life: led to believe that things are one way when in fact they are not. Disillusionment is the letdown—the feeling of betrayal and promises broken. It is important to get a feeling for setups if we are to appreciate how terrible we feel when we are let down and to recognize that the phase of breaking down is part of the healing process of regaining a sense of our own integrity.

Setups

"Gee, this is it! This is the real thing! Our love is the greatest since Romeo and Juliet. How romantic!"

"The new job has oodles of benefits and there are company parties every week! Fantastic!"

"There are shuffleboard, tennis, and racquetball courts as well as golf courses, heated swimming pools and midnight dancing in Sun City. Incredible!"

"There's a piece of land in Florida going for a song. Sounds like heaven on earth! And the person who's selling it is so charming!"

"Where there's a will there's a way!"

"If you put your mind to it, you can do anything!"

"A loving God will protect us from all harm!"

The real thing! Charming! Romantic! Incredible! Captivating! Enchanting! The setup can be understood actively and passively. Ordinarily we speak of *being* set-up—that is, passively. It is something that happens to us. Expressions like "taken in," "suckered," "caught up," "seduced," "tricked," "conned," "captivated," and "enchanted" reflect this passive side of the setup. We get caught up with our work, for example. Or we are taken in by a fast-talking salesperson, taken for a ride by a con artist. A powerful personality like David Koresh seduces us into doing what we wouldn't normally do.

Less obvious, and so more subtle, is our active collaboration in the setup. Without being conscious of it, we collude with the forces setting us up. Idols fascinate and hold our attention, but only because at some level we actively yearn to give ourselves over to someone or something. We may act coy, cute, or seductive towards the person who is leading us on. Sometimes we go looking for trouble and, when we find it, accuse someone else of setting us up. A Japanese adage expresses the active-passive nature of the set up. "First the man takes a drink. Then the drink takes a drink. Then the drink takes the man." It isn't all that rational, of course. Certainly the drink takes the man, but only because he's ready and willing to go wherever the drink wants to take him.

Our willingness to be set up can be explained only by understanding how the setup satisfies our need for meaning. The object of our fascination is something we believe can center us and give direction to our lives. Think of a man who has fallen in love and how he yearns for nothing else but to be with the woman of his dreams. Wherever he goes, whatever he does, and whoever he sees all become occasions for celebrating her. Think, too, of addicts and how the object of addiction dominates their lives. The fix could be food, alcohol, drugs, sex, or work. Whatever it is, it is crucial to their existence; Without it they fall apart; with it their lives seem to hold together—at least for a while. Yet sooner or later the bubble bursts, and the setup turns into a letdown.

Letdown

"How could you have done this? How could I have been so stupid as to have fallen for you? Couldn't I see what was happening?"

"I had no idea. They led me to believe that I didn't need to worry about job security. Then, boom! I'm fired!"

"You raise your kids, give them the shirt off your back, and then they forget about you."

"So this is it? This is retirement? I've waited all my life for this? Walking all morning in a shopping mall? And rocking my life away the rest of the day?"

If we have been led to believe parents are perfect, we learn one day that dad cheats on his income tax. Or if we marry and think our partner the ideal mate, we discover she or he isn't all that perfect. "Well, I thought at least *you'd* understand," we complain bitterly to an uncomprehending partner. Life holds promise at eighteen, but at midlife it seems empty and flat. Finally, when we retire, we are given a gold-plated pen, a chicken dinner, and a sendoff to Retirement Park Village, where we are bored silly. We are disenchanted. We've been had, betrayed! Betrayal is like jumping from the top of the stairs, expecting that someone we trust will be at the bottom to catch us—and no one's there. We end up broken and bleeding. To feel betrayed is to feel abandoned, dumped, used.

A brief description of a romantic involvement will enable us to follow the movement from setup to letdown in the life of someone who has fallen in love. It will also serve as the basis for a reflection on those "negative" feelings that so many of us harbor in the process of breaking down.

When two people fall in love, they see in one another the fulfillment of each other's dreams. These idealizations preclude noticing each other's shortcomings or annoying mannerisms. Even if they notice one another's limitations, they are conveniently forgotten or interpreted favorably. She admires him as a man of strong convictions and doesn't notice how opinionated he is. He adores her genteel qualities but is blind to her mousy demeanor.

Friends are more apt to notice the limitations the lovers don't see. The lovers dote on one another, think of one another when they are apart, and can hardly wait to be in one another's presence. The fascination with which they approach one another has a holy, otherworldly quality. And not only does each become a sacred shrine or center for the other, but each finds his or her center in the other. Is it any wonder that people who invest themselves in each other prefer not to entertain the possibility of being betrayed? When someone is betrayed in an intimate relationship, the betrayed is not only abandoned by the other but feels bereft of a self still emotionally invested in the other.

It's no surprise, then, that when the idol begins to break down, people will do whatever they can to shore it up. Even as it becomes clearer each day that they have been let down, they still want to believe otherwise. There must be an explanation! If the lover doesn't answer phone calls, it's because she is sick or out of town. But suppose she has been seen several times with another man within the last couple of days? Feeling threatened and hurt, the betrayed one continues to wait for an explanation. Of course, he is dying to call and ask for one, but he hesitates because if he does call, his suspicions might be confirmed, and he prefers the uncertainty of not knowing to the certainty that their relationship is over. Better to keep the illusion in place. She has his soul, after all. However, as he hears more and more rumors about her affair, he gathers enough courage to phone her. He still hesitates to ask her the important question. He talks about everything else, the weather, movies, TV. Only when she tells him she is seeing someone else does he speak up. In the weeks ahead he oscillates between wanting to end the relationship and figuring ways in which they might get back together again.

Reactions: Potential Problems

As relationships go, it is possible to react in any number of ways. Reactions to betrayal are normal, and while they appear to leave us broken, some of them can actually assist in the healing process. First, let's look at the problems these reactions might create and then let's examine their potential for healing.[3]

Revenge. Revenge is wanting to get even and destroy the other, wanting to hurt someone as deeply as we have been hurt. An eye for an eye, a tooth for a tooth. While it is a normal reaction, our desire for revenge can become so obsessive that we injure ourselves in the effort to get even. The obsession absorbs our energy so that we can't think of anything else. It upsets us that the person responsible for hurting us seems remarkably free of guilt and remorse for what was done.

Depreciation. Another reaction to betrayal is depreciation. If in our setups we idolize, angelize, and idealize the object of our fascination, in the letdown we demonize the other. What we formerly regarded as ideal, we now consider irredeemably flawed. Whereas in the setup the other could do no wrong, now wrong is the only thing the other can do. Not only do we see what is undesirable in the other, we project our own negative qualities onto the other.

While the language we use to describe the object of our enchantment is characteristically inflationary (the other is superhuman, divine, etc.), the language of disillusionment is deflationary (the other is subhuman, demonic, etc.) What was a beauty mark becomes an ugly wart. The lover who endlessly recited a litany of praises for his beloved now endlessly gives a breakdown of her faults. If his friends had unsuccessfully noted his lover's arrogance while he was still enchanted, in his disenchantment she is arrogance personified. Previously oblivious of any of her shadowy traits, now he notices only the shadow.

What he doesn't notice is that he is also projecting his own inadequacies onto her. For example, he sidesteps his refusal to assume responsibility for his life by accusing her of having prevented him from making important decisions. He faults her for not understanding him ("Well, I thought *you'd* understand!"). But he himself is lacking in self-understanding. *Cynicism.* Cynicism is another reaction to disillusionment. Having gotten burned in one situation, cynics generalize that all similar situations will lead to similar results. For example, if a man has cheated on a woman, then she may conclude all men are cheats. Or if one bishop is found out to be a liar, then they are all liars. And if one politician is corrupt, they all must be. The cynic's response to betrayal is never to trust again. Having been deeply hurt, they believe trusting again will simply lead to more pain. Consequently, cynicism becomes a defensive posture to prevent further hurt.

Cynics not only see through the lens of their overvaluations of a person, place, or institution, they tend to generalize from the overvaluations. In other words, cynics undervalue or deflate most everything in the phase of disillusionment. Nothing is worthwhile. Nobody is all that good. Everything is phony and unreal. Whatever others hold valuable, cynics perceive to be sham or questionable.

Self-rejection. One of the most potentially destructive reactions to betrayal is self-rejection. It is one thing to feel rejected by someone; it is quite another to reject ourselves. In self-rejection we deny some important aspect of ourselves, usually the side of ourselves where we had been most open and vulnerable to the one who has betrayed us. Think of two people who for months have been exchanging love letters. They disclose things they have never revealed to anyone else. Then one of the partners feels betrayed as the love letters in which she had bared her soul are returned. She rereads the letters and mutters, "How could I have said these things? This is ridiculous. This isn't me! I must have been out of my mind when I wrote these."

Self-rejection, like cynicism, is a defense mechanism. If being tender has led to suffering, we determine never to be tender again. Or if being truthful has caused rejection, we promise ourselves never to tell another what we honestly think. Unfortunately our wounds are never healed solely by anesthetizing ourselves to pain. Disclaiming what is most tender, caring, or truthful, in ourselves is equivalent to burying what is special about who we are. On the other hand, telling ourselves, "But this is me and I will not deny it," is painful but life affirming.

Paranoia. Becoming paranoid—another reaction to betrayal— is an attempt to prevent further rejections by establishing the rules for future relationships. This is a form of control in which we insist that the partner in a new relationship promise "in blood" that he or she won't let happen what the previous partner had done. Never again can there be room for promises breached! However, interpersonal relationships not based on mutual trust do not invite mutual self-disclosure and consequently cannot develop in any meaningful way. Having been severely hurt and fearful of being hurt again, we tend to "seal up" and become excessively guarded and suspicious in our relationships.

Shame. Finally, what is devastating is the intense shame a betrayed person can experience. The potential for shame increases to the extent that the individual has suffered from shame very early in life as a result of perceived rejection at the hand of a parent or a parent surrogate. Psychologists have pointed out that if we have never experienced much self-esteem in our lives, then we are particularly vulnerable to later assaults on our sense of self. The reaction to this assault is rage. Rage serves as a protective shell to prevent further shaming. Some of us simply will never trust again because we have been so deeply shamed.

Reactions: Potential for Healing

It is important for us to appreciate the fact that as negative as these reactions feel, all of them serve to protect a fragile self from future harm by giving us the needed time to recover from the breakdown that occurred. In some instances the reactions can be helpful in reclaiming our individuality, gaining perspective on unquestioned assumptions, and appreciating people and things independently of needs and expectations.

Depreciation. In depreciation the tendency to regard the other person as a demon may be the first step in gaining a sense of our own separateness. If we have relied too excessively on others, been too dependent on them for our sense of self, if we have defined ourselves solely on the basis of our relationship with another, then we may have to experience the

other as mean and devious in order to separate psychologically. Only then can we claim our center, which we had unconsciously handed over to and discovered only in the other.

We may have first to denounce, deny, and denigrate
someone we had idolized, because we are still very attached
to and dependent on that person. We make all kinds of negative projections in order to regain the self we had invested in
the other. Our own self-interest is at stake, and if we view
interest as energy, then the other, as the carrier of that
energy, has to be symbolically slain or broken open if we are
to regain the energy. For example, adolescents sometimes
need to see their parents as ogres to fight, because their
reliance on these all-providers prevents them from striking
out on their own and discovering that they too are potentially
all-providers.

Of course, depreciating the other ought to move to a
new phase: seeing that what we denied was not only the
other's limitations, imperfections, peccadilloes, and idiosyn-
crasies but our own shadow or negative side revealed in the
other. We have to recognize how we have demonized the
other with our own demons, that what we don't like in them is
amplified by our own negative traits.

Cynicism. The cynical reaction that nothing is worthwhile,
nobody is all that good, can also lead us to the realization
that nothing or nobody is God. A creative cynicism sees God
by denying the reality of God in any and every idol made to
look like God. "Vanity of vanities and all is vanity," is the
response of the truly religious person who, like the cynic,
sees through illusions.

It is possible to summarize the preceding considera-
tions about setups and letdowns by reflecting on the diagram. On the left end of the line is the Self, and on the right,
the Other. What we would expect between adults would be a

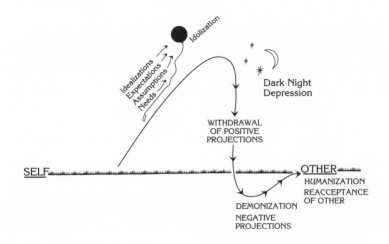

simple act of regard, a simple act of seeing. "Hi, this is me" and "So that's you" illustrated in the broken base line. But things are never so simple. Unable to accept ourselves fully, we project. During the phase of enchantment we project our needs, idealizations, expectations, and assumptions onto the other until, at the top of the curve, we have made of the other an idol, that is, overvalued, angelized, or whatever.

But the other cannot bear our projections indefinitely. During the phase of disillusionment we withdraw positive projections. As the curve moves downward, it plummets below the line of normal seeing, and the other becomes the target of our negative projections. Here we demonize or undervalue the other. The entire decline is also a depressing time because we are suffering from loss, the loss of illusion.

Finally, in the best scenario, the curve gradually moves upward to meet the other on the broken baseline. This is the humanizing phase, during which we reappropriate ourselves and reaccept the other. It is the time of withdrawing negative projections and seeing the other as he or she is, not as saint or sinner but as saint-sinner, as a human being. Equally important, we accept ourselves as saint-sinner, as fully human. We see and accept ourselves and one another on an equal basis.

The Problem of Forgiveness

This diagram might also help us understand something about healing the wound of real or imagined betrayal. Strange as it seems, healing means becoming fully aware of one's reactions to betrayal as they have been described here. But wouldn't it make more sense to get on with our lives rather than dwell on all these negative feelings? And if we have been exhorted to forgive those who have hurt us, then wouldn't it be big of us to let bygones be bygones?

Regarding the first question, we can't get on with our lives by ignoring our reactions any more than we can apply a Band-Aid over a festering wound and think it has been taken care of. The healing process begins by acknowledging just how deeply we have been wounded by what has happened. Until we become aware of the pain, we cannot let go of it. Our muscles can be taut for so many years that it seems the normal state of affairs. Then at some point someone else might say, "You look like you're in pain! Why so tense?" If we become aware of our condition, then chances are the pain can be acknowledged. This doesn't mean the pain is getting worse. It means that now we can do something about it.

However, if we have been deeply hurt and ignore the pain of betrayal, then we are unconsciously motivated to seek revenge. And this brings us to the subject of forgiveness. We might feel pressures to forgive from friends who think this is the heroic thing to do or from clerics who think it's the godly thing to do. If we aren't in touch with any of the previously described reactions to betrayal, we might coolly deliberate with ourselves whether we'll let so-and-so off the hook. As we see it, the other's in the red and we're in the black. And since it's a question of the power to forgive, we're in the catbird seat. The power to forgive? The *power?*

How much rage is hidden in our self-talk as we weigh the pros and cons of forgiving? If a mother or father has made us feel like a piece of junk while growing up, how much of this assessment enters into saying, "Can I forgive? Or can't I? Is it within my power or isn't it?" But the pressure to play the hero in the arena of forgiveness takes its toll if we feel we can't manage the heroic. Then we feel guilty. "I just can't—not after what he has done to me!" Maybe it is just as well that we can't execute the coup. Otherwise we'd be gratefully flexing the muscle responsible for forgiveness.

Then is there to be no forgiveness? Yes, there is, but not the way we think. Using the previous diagram, we see that genuine forgiveness is possible only when we have withdrawn negative projections. Then we can see ourselves and the other as neither sinners nor saints but as human beings possessing both light and shadow. When we see each other on an equal basis, forgiveness is not so much a matter of one of us assuming the burden of forgiving the other as it is of simply recognizing forgiveness when it happens. Then no one need take the credit or the blame for the success or failure of forgiving. Doesn't our experience tell us that, struggle as we will, forgiving is not something we do but something that happens. No thanks to the efforts of a heroic ego! Why?

Because ultimately it is God who forgives. All that we can do is celebrate and be thankful for what has happened. It was John Patton who developed the idea that forgiveness is a discovery rather than something to be sought after.

It is from the position of being an ordinary, responsible human being that this discovery becomes possible. As those who have studied the creative process have found, we are more likely to discover something when we are not trying to prove anything.... Thus, the function of church and ministry is not to supervise acts of forgiveness, but to provide relationships in which genuine humanity, including the possibility that I am forgiving, can be discovered. Human forgiveness is something more likely to be discovered when the pastor is not trying to help someone do it. When I can recognize what is like me, i.e., neighbor-hood, in another, I have either forgiven that person or discovered that forgiveness as something done is not the main point anyway."[4]

The discovery of forgiveness is poignantly illustrated in an article written by Peter Baird, a lawyer from Texas. He described a reunion that he was to have with his eighty-year-old father, whom he hadn't seen for fifteen years. His father was an alcoholic and often violent. Since father and son were continually battling one another, they finally parted with such fury that the break seemed irreparable.

They had never gotten along with one another. His father had been a physician who was drafted into the army in World War II and shot in his surgeon's hand while in service. He had a difficult time accepting his son's close relationship with his mother. His medical practice became almost an addiction, and he suffered from periodic bouts of alcoholism, depression, and aggression. Disapproval of his son culminated during the Vietnam War when he managed to have his son drafted to fight for freedom the way he had.

Baird wondered how he would conduct himself with this man, who had refused to examine him when he was paralyzed. His father had denounced his paralysis as malingering and had stormed out of the house, leaving him to lie helplessly on the floor until his mother managed to contact another country doctor thirty miles away. The diagnosis was polio. Baird simply did not know how he could act and talk at last like a forgiving and loving son.

When they finally met one another in the reception room of the local airport in the town where his father lived, the two of them greeted one another formally. He had been warned by his father's second wife that his father was often confused and frustrated. She told him that his father probably had Alzheimer's disease. However, he hadn't wanted any kind of evaluation or treatment and got extremely angry when pressed to do something about his condition. During Baird's visit his father's erratic behavior became apparent as he confused his son with a deceased surgeon, wore a couple of wristwatches, and slipped off the rational track time after time. And in the men's room of a nearby country club, when they went for dinner, he turned away from the urinal and, while still unzipped and conspicuous, attempted to introduce him to a startled stranger who had just walked through the door.

However, to Baird's surprise his father also generated an unprecedented flow of paternal behavior. He seemed genuinely concerned about his grandchildren, his son's marriage, and his work. He was solicitous in very touching but bewildering ways: pouring his son a new drink when he already had a fresh one; writing out unintelligible prescriptions for maladies that he didn't have and that he had just invented. Then Baird writes,

> As time passed, our conversation ebbed into a long
> quiet while my father stared out the window at the
> headlights of a freight train on the opposite shore.
> Slowly, he turned to me and, with an expression

that I had never seen before but that I later took to be love, said: "I know that I wasn't much of a father to you, Peter, and that I made a lot of mistakes. I want you to know that I am very sorry." Astonished and moved by the warmth of this December thaw from an implacable man with whom I had fought all my life for approval, all I could think to say was: "That's all right, Dad. It really is O.K." And it was finally.[5]

Being Disillusioned: The Road to Maturity

One of the most comprehensive attempts to explain the necessity of setups and letdowns in a person's development from a psychological perspective comes from the work of the late Heinz Kohut, the founder of "self psychology." His approach also illustrates the contributions of breaking up and breaking down in the life of the infant. He theorized that the infant depends on a "mirroring other" and an "idealized other" as external sources for developing some sense of a self. The mirroring other reflects back to the infant its sense of greatness—what we might call the "wow" effect. The "Wow, you're great!" in the oohs and aahs of the mother's delight in her child becomes the child's "Wow, I'm great!" and the precursor of "self-wowing," that is, self-admiration. Inadequate mirroring of the child's worth means the child as adult will be forever looking to others for the self-validation he or she never received as a child.

On the other hand, the idealized other is the seemingly omnipotent other whom the child esteems, admires, and looks up to and whose strength the child needs to merge with. In so doing, the other's strength becomes temporarily available to the child. Gradually, the idealized other is transformed into the internal ideals and aspirations that inspire and guide the child into maturity. The failure of the other to be the ideal leaves the child devoid of an idealized other to internalize and appropriate. Without any internal ideals the child grows up needing to be attached to an idealized other (a rock star, guru, politician, etc.) to feel competent.

Assimilating both the idealized other as one's own ideals and the mirroring other as self-admiring or self-esteeming is what ultimately constitutes a core self for the growing child. Only a child so endowed can more and more provide for itself what initially only the parents could provide.

This process is never painless. Appropriating the admiring other as self-admiration and the idealized other as internalized ideals can't take place unless the child experiences some letdown or failure by the parents. This failure is the breakdown of the "perfect" rapport with the parent. For example, the mother may be unable to give the infant food at the very moment the infant is crying for it. But the child expects all its needs to be satisfied whenever and wherever those needs are expressed. However good the mother is, she is never perfect from the infant's perspective. Adequate mothering doesn't require perfection. But for the infant anything less than perfection leads to the experience of the breakdown, without which there would be no motivation to internalize ideals and become independent.

For Kohut the self comes into existence only as the result of what we call the letdowns. Consequently, letdowns contribute positively to self development. Put simply, the child looks to the parents to be everything while gradually discovering through many mini-letdowns that they aren't. Simultaneously, the child is forced to compensate by internalizing the parental functions and thus develops a self structure. This process of internalizing these functions is the child's creative way of "breaking up" the parents as psychological nutrients in developing a self. Thus, the child learns

self-soothing as a result of the parents' not always being able
to be there to soothe. Were the parent always present, the
child would have no need to appropriate the soothing function of the mother. Or if the parent were always present to
admire and extol the child, then the child would be forever
dependent on others for esteem needs. The letdowns, or
moments of "optimal frustrations," as Kohut called them,
become opportune moments for the child to mature.

The End of Illusions?

Do we learn from our setups and letdowns? If learning
means that we arrive at a point in our lives when we no
longer suffer illusions, then we might as well give up on learning. This side of the grave it is always possible to create idols.
Given our intense longing to find our heart's fulfillment, the
denial of the possibility or even the likelihood of creating
idols seems itself to be an illusion.

However, if by learning we mean that our experience
with previous illusions might teach us how vulnerable we are
and how quickly we can get attached to our illusions, then we
might learn to become more attentive to whatever is beginning to captivate and hold fast our hearts. Yet attention
ought not to be construed as wide-eyed vigilance but rather
as attending to people and things.

This attending is a gentle regard for people in and for
themselves. We might call this kind of attention a contemplative attitude. We shall have more to say about this attitude
later, but here we should note that contemplation, in reference to our illusions, means that we become aware of them
but do not engage in aggressive attempts to eradicate them.
If we are determined to destroy illusions by a frontal assault,
we give them a power they don't deserve. Obviously, the
alcoholic's love affair with the bottle means the bottle's significance has been inflated beyond its worth. But demonizing

the bottle or attributing to it every evil in creation is another form of inflation (albeit negative) that holds its own form of fascination. We can be as attached to what we intensely dislike as we had been attached to what we had previously loved. Any person going through a divorce know this. And unfortunately, some people who have been divorced for years are still negatively attached to ex-spouses demonized beyond recognition!

But there is more to address in breaking down than disillusionment. There is very often depression that weighs so heavily on the soul as to leave one feeling broken.

Chapter 3

Breaking Down:
Depression's Bad Press

> Midway this way of life we're bound upon,
> I woke to find myself in a dark wood,
> Where the right road was wholly lost and gone.[1]
>
> Dante

Closely related to disillusionment is depression. Being depressed, more than being disillusioned, is an experience many of us would prefer not acknowledging. Yet like disillusionment, depression can serve a constructive purpose. Before we consider depression's potential, we ought to examine our negative attitude towards depression.

A Bad Press

The obvious reason we dislike being depressed is that it makes us feel miserable. When we are engaged in our world we *ex*press who we are, that is, our energies are focused outwards. Fully engaged, we leave our mark or impact on our world. We are present to others in and through the decisions we make. But when we are *de*pressed, our energies are no longer available as *ex*pressions of who we are. Rather we feel the weight of being pressed in. We feel emotionally spent, broke! No longer do we feel engaged or committed to our world. Instead we feel aloof, indifferent, removed. Decisions that formerly were easy to make are now difficult. We find ourselves stuck on dead center. We cannot move, or we do so only with difficulty.

For example, when we shop for food, even the simplest decisions are a chore. We look at the white bread and the brown bread on the shelf, and we wonder which bread we shall buy. We stand there for fifteen minutes trying to decide, while five other people come by and seem to have no problem deciding what kind of bread they want. Frustrated, we finally leave with no bread!

Depression as a Disease

Another set of reasons why we harbor negative impressions about depression are cultural. We think of depression as some alien power that enters us and needs to be eliminated. Like the measles or the mumps it needs to be treated so we can be normal again. We assume depression is an abnormal condition, a disease, which interferes with being normal.

But as Lesley Hazleton[2] has pointed out, we assume not only that it is abnormal but that it isn't the "right" way to be. There is something wrong with us if we are depressed. After all, don't we have the right to be happy? And if we are happy, aren't we all right? By identifying "unhappy" with wrong and "happy" with right, we are making moral judgments about these states of being. And of course if being unhappy is wrong, we must have done something to be wrong. Is it any wonder that we might feel terribly guilty about being so unhappy when we are depressed?

The idea that depression is always a disease, is something bad, or has no right to exist doesn't mean that a depressed person is going to take the necessary steps to deal constructively with the "problem." On the contrary, being depressed might lead to even more depression! We can understand this predicament if we recall times when someone has counseled us when we were worrying or anxious,

"Don't worry! There's nothing to worry about!" or "You have nothing to be anxious about!" Our response might have been to worry more because we were worrying or to be more anxious about being so anxious. The last thing we need is for well-intentioned people to tell us that we ought not to be going through what we are going through. Their advice is as helpful as telling a person who stutters, "Don't stutter!" That simply intensifies the bind the stutterer is in.

How then are we to understand depression if not as an illness or something that is wrong or bad? First, it needs to be clearly stated that what follows does not apply to persons who are severely depressed and in need of medication to alleviate their suffering. Nor does my characterization of depression mean that no medical attention or counseling would be helpful. Often it is necessary to get medication and counseling as well as fresh perspectives on the meaning of depression. But increasingly there are psychiatrists and psychologists who recognize that depression need not be understood in a completely negative light. It is often an appropriate response in people who find themselves in certain sets of circumstances. As with disillusionment, depression too has its place in the life cycle. Without depression we cannot mature as persons, nor would our spiritual journey have much depth.

Depression and Loss

Depression is connected with loss. The most obvious kind of loss is the loss associated with death. We might not literally lose someone to death, but we can suffer any number of losses in a lifetime, and each involves some kind of dying. We lose friends, lovers, husbands, wives, jobs, homes. And whatever the loss, mourning is always appropriate. It is the time of breaking away, of saying good-bye. We mourn not only for the loss of the other but also for whatever of ourselves has gone with the other. It isn't only the other that dies. In *Loss and Change,* Peter Marris writes, "The fundamental crisis of bereavement arises, not from the loss of others, but the loss of self."[3] Something of us that the other has brought alive in our relationship has died. This double loss accounts for the feeling of emptiness that we experience with the other's departure. It also accounts for our reluctance to let go of the other. No other person will be able to call to life that special something of ourselves in the same way in which the lost other has done.

Frequently, we also need to mourn the loss of illusions or sets of assumptions we hold about others and ourselves. We have already seen how we idealize and idolize others. One morning we wake up to discover the death (literally or figuratively) of those idols. But what we haven't considered are the expectations we place upon ourselves.

Often what we expect of ourselves are simply the expectations that others have of us and that we have then internalized. Here "others" refers to family, peers, culture. We are told to do the best we can with our lives, but the pressure is to achieve, to be successful, to be a winner. After all, we think that we are "entitled" to be successful and happy at home and in the workplace. But what happens when we succeed at home but not at work or at work but not at home? Or, God forbid, when we succeed neither at home nor at work? We have then failed ourselves! The number of people out of work is staggering, and while it is frequently through no fault of their own, the personal sense of failure is tremendous. Why? Because if we are entitled, if we have a right to succeed, then failure points to our being defective or inadequate. Self-esteem plummets, and the result is depression. Others reap the benefits of success, and this—the breach between them and us—simply highlights our failure.

Depression as a Sign

Within the context of transitions, it is possible to understand depression as a sign indicating something about personal development and/or spiritual transformation. While it might be difficult for a depressed person or for a counselor to identify the meaning of the depression, knowing whether it is a matter of personal development or spiritual development can give a deeper appreciation of the value of depression in transitional experiences. Certainly the realization that depression need not be interpreted as a disease is itself an advance in our understanding of depression. What does depression tell us about personal and/or spiritual development?

In her book on depression, Janice Wetzel offers the following description of depression:

> I suggest that depression is like fever, not a disease in itself, but a warning signal indicating that the growth process has been blocked. Barriers may loom up as gridirons of environmentally imposed limitations, or as obstructions representing inner conflicts that inhibit development. In either case, depression is an intrinsic medium of communication within the body, inextricably linked to development. Demands for a dimension of development that are incongruent with one's existing structural needs end in depression. The same phenomenon occurs when one's inner psychological structure is developed at a given level. Depression in such cases is a biochemical manifestation of pressure toward further growth. We must listen to depression, then, and respect its message.[4]

We break out into depression as we would a fever. But depression is not a disease in itself. According to Wetzel, depression is a sign that draws attention to some area of our lives that needs tending. There are issues or themes through-out the life cycle that need to be negotiated and renegotiated, and depression is a warning signal that we are either neglect-ing work that needs to be done or that we are going about it in the wrong way. Without this warning we might not change ideas, attitudes, and behaviors responsible for retarding or pre-maturely forcing psychological growth. Among the themes in our lives that need to be addressed repeatedly are negative and positive connections and negative and positive aloneness. Negative connections and aloneness give rise to depression.

Negative Connections

All of us need the approval and acceptance of others. We need these from a very early age. Our sense of being valued is first validated by our parents. They mirror to us that we are worthwhile. Initially our self-esteem is based on their admiring words, glances, gestures, embraces. There is nothing wrong with this. Not unless our self-worth is brokered *solely* through the approval of others. If whatever we do in life we do to gain and maintain others' acceptance, there is a problem. If we don't derive any satisfaction from our work or play unless we are first pleasing others, then, too, there is a problem.

If we chronically ask questions like, "Do you like it? Do the others like it? Does God like what I am doing?" this reliance on others leads to depression. Even the anticipation of losing an external source of gratification can generate depression. But notice that depression in these instances is not a disease. It is a signal alerting us that our way of relating to others isn't healthy. Without this breaking news, we would continue business as usual to the detriment of our psychic well-being.

Our sole source of gratification could be either a domi-nant other or a dominant goal. Early in life we can become overly compliant in our reliance on a parent or parent substitute as the source of acceptance. "I'll do handstands just to get your love. Say you'll love me and I'll do whatever you want, even if deep down what you want is contrary to what I want." The dominant other becomes our lifeline, which we cling to at any cost. The problem arises when we are upset or angry at this lifeline. Then we can't easily express our anger for fear of losing the lifeline we so desperately need. Unexpressed anger, whether felt toward the lifeline or toward ourselves for being so dependent, contributes to our depression.

This overreliance on the acceptance of others might be even more crucial if we need it to avoid the feeling of being evil or wicked. It is one thing to seek another's approval so we won't be regarded as inefficient or lazy; it is another thing to desire it so we won't feel dirty and guilty about ourselves before God. The messages many of us get very early from parents or parent surrogates is that we are dirty, for example, for playing with or exposing our genitals or innocently muttering an obscenity. These are essentially religious messages. They are religious either because they are associated with the only gods who matter, our parents, or because we are told that God doesn't like us and will punish us for being bad. Associating what parents want of us with what God wants makes us feel as anxious about getting God's approval as it does about pleasing our parents. Such impressions are deep and long lasting. No wonder so many adults find little comfort hearing from the pulpit that God loves them. Religious messages can leave us feeling more broken than healed.

The dominant other in our lives can change as we grow older. Instead of a parent, a wife or husband can become the dominant other. We then depend on that other as a source of gratification. We do whatever pleases a spouse so as to retain the spouse's approval or prevent the spouse's abandoning us. In the process who we are is increasingly shaped and defined by what the other wants from us or what we perceive the other wants. Whatever our own deepest needs are, we do not express them because we are fearful of losing our spouse's love. In those rare moments when we are doing what we really enjoy doing, we might also begin to feel guilty because it doesn't seem to satisfy our partner's needs or wishes. In many marriages the dominant other is the man. The dependent wife relies on him for her sense of self. In her book on women and depression, *Silencing the Self,* Dana Crowley Jack has pointed out that the woman who doesn't find a voice to express her own self-needs doesn't have a self. Her self has been silenced.

Why is the man ordinarily the dominant other and the woman the dependent one in the relationship? From early on, the boy has been encouraged to differentiate from the other, the first other being a woman, his mother. He has been encouraged to be on his own, achieve and get ahead in the world. The same cannot be said for the little girl. Traditionally the young woman has been encouraged to marry and settle down with a husband whose future could become hers. Her own dreams are put on hold. Her aspirations for her own development are set aside to further his. She is to find her identity through her husband. Jean Baker Miller *(Toward a New Psychology of Women)* has written that a woman's appreciation of her own separateness, talents, gifts, and dreams doesn't come easily, since her self-definition is as one who looks after and nurtures others. To the extent that she is a giver and cares for others, she is acceptable to herself. The idea that a woman might define herself through developing talents not directly related to the nurturing role is alien and threatening to many women and men.[5]

The dominant goal has traditionally been a man's concern. It is his work, his job that concerns him. His sense of himself is tied to his work. His self-definition is partially linked with his need for others' approval in the workplace. Failure associated with work is more likely to devastate a man than it is a woman. Often men who are out of work feel worthless, and as their self-esteem plummets, they get depressed.

The kind of depression associated with failure to achieve satisfaction solely through the dominant other or the dominant goal is the result of negative connections. As Robert Kegan reminds us, we all have a need to be connected, but we also have a need to have an identity and differentiate from our parents, from the people we work with, from the church, from our children. Excessive reliance on others at any point in the life cycle is unhealthy, and depression is the warning signal.

Negative Aloneness

If depression in people with negative connections illustrates failure to differentiate from others and to experience a sense of self-worth and value independently of others, then depression in loners illustrates the failure of people to relate to others at all. To be relational is to be available physically, emotionally, and spiritually to oneself and to others. The degree of availability to others obviously depends on whether the other is a spouse, parent, child, friend, or stranger. Availability is another way of speaking about intimacy. Our capacity to connect to our own feelings, aspirations, hopes, or fears is essential to connecting with what others are feeling, hoping for, or fearing.

It is remarkable how many people cannot answer a simple question like, "Tell me how you feel?" They have been so unavailable to their feelings for so long they do not know what they are feeling. Actually, this should not strike us as surprising. How many of us have grown up being told "You shouldn't feel that way! That's not right!" or "You shouldn't even think such thoughts—they're dirty!" We learn our lesson so well that even before we've had a chance to feel what we are feeling or permit ourselves to picture what it is that needs to be imagined, we censor our feelings, thoughts, and fantasies. Then one day as adults we find ourselves going to the psychiatrist because something is going on inside of us that we cannot deal with. And what does the psychiatrist tell us? "Free associate! It will be helpful if you could tell me what you are feeling and thinking!" And of course, we might be paying $150 an hour to become available to all the feeling we have censored for so many years.

Men more than women have a problem relating. Men are often conditioned to regard any kind of dependency as feminine and not masculine. It isn't manly to cry or express feelings of tenderness. So men learn to wear masks and pretend not to need or not to be hurt when they really are. While this is more of a problem for men it is not simply a gender issue. From very early both boys and girls become "parentified children."

"Parentified children" have never been permitted to be children in the first place. They have had to be parents to their own parents by trying to meet a parent's narcissistic needs. They did this by denying their own needs. Theirs was a role reversal at a very early age. Concealing their own needs, they focused on nurturing their parents. These are the children who often grow up to become the caregivers in our society: clergy, nurses, physicians, and psychotherapists. These people frequently come from backgrounds in which they learned that their survival depended on being sensitive to others' moods, for example, those of an alcholic father or mother.

The consequence of being sensitive to others' needs and oblivious to one's own is chronic low-grade depression. Sufferers from this condition are unhappy people who have no idea what it is like to enjoy life. But again, the low-grade depression is a symptom—like a fever, it signifies the need for a change in outlook or direction. Only when they express their dependency needs can healing take place. It isn't enough to nurture others. They have often been doing this for years. Are they able to receive nurturing? That is the real issue.

Generally speaking, women have developed their relational skills more than men. This is revealed in later life when the incidence of depression is much higher among men than it is among women.[6] Men, like women, have relational needs. But they have concealed these needs not only from others but from themselves by pretending they were strong and independent. However, in old age the defenses crumble, revealing a fragile, vulnerable person. Sadly, a lot of older men have buddies, but they do not have friends to whom they can unburden themselves. Older women, on the other hand, are less vulnerable to depression than at any other time in the adult life cycle, since their capacity for empathy and relationship is more highly developed.

Depression and Developmental Transitions

We can also see the significance of depression in what Robert Kegan has written about its appearance in developmental transitions.[7] As we saw in chapter 2, when we are living between identities (between not and not-not), we are experiencing the dual loss of understanding self and world. This constitutes the loss of meaning. And it is this loss that is expressed and signified in depression. What the depression doesn't signify is that something is "wrong" with us.

The specific kind of depression we experience in a transition depends on the nature of the transition. For example, in discussing the developmental transition from the socializing self to the self-authorizing self, Kegan describes this loss as the loss of a self that is special to us because of our perceived likability in the eyes of others. We had known ourselves to be agreeable and nice in contrast with a newly emerging self that feels cold and indifferent. However, in retrospect, feelings of anger at the old self for having been so compliant contribute to the particular kind of depression we experience.

The transition from the self-authorizing self to an inter-dependent self is accompanied by a depression in which we feel the loss of a self that is special because it is self-con-tained, controlled, and in charge. But anger at this same self for being remote and isolated in its self-containment also contributes to the depression. Moreover, the newly emerging self's openness to others' belief systems, moral perspectives, and truths generates contradictory feelings on the one hand, of being out of control, wicked, and decadent and, on the other,of ecstasy in a newfound freedom.

Depression, then, is not an abnormal condition as we go through developmental transitions. However, depression can become unnecessarily severe if we resist the movement of our own development as a person. As we evolve, we natu-rally experience anxiety and depression because our world, as we have known and lived in it, is collapsing. But resisting its collapse through rigid defenses and maneuvers makes the transition more difficult than it need be.

In this circumstance psychotherapy might be neces-sary, because we may lack a supportive network of relation-ships to provide the "natural therapy" needed to negotiate the transition. By natural therapy Kegan means the kind of affir-mation and challenge that family, parents, spouse, friends might give us as we go through the transition. These support-ive networks or holding communities will be described later.

Suicide and Depression

The dangers of misinterpreting the meaning of depres-sion in transitions ought not to be underestimated. If the loss of meaning or the inability to make sense out of life leads us to the conclusion that life is pointless, suicide might seem to be the only viable option of breaking out of this unhappy state. However, it is only a perspective on life or a way of understanding ourselves and our world that needs to die. It would be tragic if we mistakenly were to interpret depression as a call to complete self-destruction.

In his book *Transforming Depression,* Jungian analyst David Rosen theorizes that we need to distinguish between putting to death a crippling perspective on life, one that brings its own kind of death, and literally ending one's life. The former he calls egocide in contrast to the latter, suicide.[8] In his experience many people are depressed because of a self-destructive attitude towards life that is intimately tied up with the ego, or sense of I-ness. The connection between ego and attitude constitutes the ego identity. The people he describes had attempted suicide but fortunately failed in the attempt and came to understand that it was a perspective on life, not life itself, that had to be terminated.

For many people what is destructive is a crippling self-image that constitutes the ego identity. Egocide refers to the symbolic killing of whatever in the ego, or I, has contributed to low self-esteem—for example, a punitive, harsh, judgmental attitude towards oneself. What also often needs to be slain is a parental introject or representation that has contributed to the construction of the ego's crippling aspect. These representations are the internal residues of a mother or father who had been cold, insensitive, or abusive. The whole process is painful because the person needs to let go of something in himself that has shaped his ego identity.

Like any loss, letting go involves grieving over the loss. Symbolically in dreams or art therapy one slays the crippling figure associated with the negative self-image. Even though egocide is based on letting only a part of the ego die, it feels like total ego death, and during the transition one feels dead. Egocide illustrates a contemporary rite of passage in which spiritual transformation occurs only through the death of what had been intimately identified with one's self.

Egocide often needs to take place in major transitions. Even in a situation where the ego identity, governed by a dominant ego image, is appropriate and healthy at one stage of development, it might become inappropriate at another. For example, adolescents need psychically to kill off and let go of a dominant ego image and identity tied up with inner parental images or representations. Ideally the adolescent would transform the parental image into his or her own ego image and unique identity. What is disturbing in Rosen's book is the idea that so many young people have succeeded in committing suicide when egocide was what actually was called for. Another Jungian analyst, Robert Moore, maintains a position similar to Rosen's. He writes in *The Magician Within* that the suicide's ego has misunderstood

> the call of the Self to die to its old ways of being, feeling, and thinking. In the absence of a spiritual sense of how to hear the call, the Ego takes the message literally. Unable to withstand devastating unconscious pressures to end the Ego's present orientation—which the Ego may regard as the only possible way of living—an individual may end his own life.[9]

What is so troubling for people going through transitions in our society is that there are so few mentors to assist them with spiritual transformation. And because of the absence of people to guide others through transitions, it "is not so surprising that suicide rates are highest among teenagers and the elderly. These two periods of life, perhaps more than any others, are times of upheaval and transition."[10]

Moore's focus in his book is on men's transitional experiences that correspond with rites of passage. As in his other books he fruitfully explores the liminal phase and is guided in that exploration by Turner's studies on liminality. He refers to the liminal phase as being "in the belly of the whale." The liminal period is a time for dealing with painful memories, unresolved childhood developmental issues, and other unfinished business. He interprets these transitional experiences to be initiations into richer, deeper, more mature ways of being human. They are precipitated by major life cycle changes or by some kind of trauma such as a divorce.

Although Moore rarely refers explicitly to depression in these transitions, he doesn't need to. His characterization of the liminal phase as equivalent to the "dark night of the soul" suggests depression as part of the experience. And his description of liminal space certainly tells us something about disillusionment and the vision born out of the death of illusions. "It dissolves our previous expectations as to ways of experiencing ourselves and our relationship to the world. Then it offers us a new vision of ourselves and our relationships."[11]

Thomas Moore's chapter on depression in his book *Care of the Soul,* a chapter he calls "Gifts of Depression," is a thoughtful reflection on depression's possibilities. As a psychotherapist he is well-acquainted with how painful and debilitating depression can become. But he thinks that depression has a necessary role to play. Some feelings and thoughts seem to emerge only in a dark mood. If the mood is suppressed, then so are their attendant ideas and reflections. Just as expressions of affection are important for the emotions of love, depression may be an important channel for valuable negative feelings.

Moore thinks that we might appreciate the role of depression if we could purge its negative connotations and simply recognize depression as a state of being, neither bad nor good, rather than a problem that needs to be eradicated. Why, he asks, do we always feel life has to be joyful? He suggests that perhaps we have to broaden our vision and see that feelings of emptiness, the loss of familiar understandings and structures in life, and the vanishing of enthusiasm, even though they seem negative, are elements that can be appropriated and used to give life fresh imagination. Depression, he tells us,

> grants the gift of experience...as an attitude toward yourself. You get a sense of having lived through something, of being older and wiser. You know that life is suffering, and that knowledge makes a difference. You can't enjoy the bouncy, carefree innocence of youth any longer, a realization that entails both sadness because of the loss, and pleasure in a new feeling of self-acceptance and self-knowledge. This awareness of age has a halo of melancholy around it, but it also enjoys a measure of nobility.[12]

Moore's association of depression and disillusionment is a succinct summary of the relationship between them.

> People of all ages sometimes say from their depression that life is over, that their hopes for the future have proved unfounded. They are disillusioned because the values and understandings by which they have lived for years suddenly make no sense....Care of the soul requires acceptance of all this dying. The temptation is to champion our familiar ideas about life right up to the last second, but it may be necessary in the end to give them up, to enter into the movement of death. If the symptom is felt as the sense that life is over, and that there's no use in going on, then an affirmative approach to this feeling might be a conscious, artful giving-in to the emotions and thoughts of ending that depression has stirred up.[13]

Depression and disillusionment often go hand in hand in our experiences of breaking down. Disillusionment is the result of the loss of illusions, and depression is intimately connected with loss. The strength of the illusion and the subsequent disillusionment might indicate the intensity and duration of the depression. Depression and disillusionment often signal the dark night in which one is confronting illusions, becoming "purified" of them, and coming to a progressively better understanding of oneself in relation to oneself and the world. Just as there are possibilities in depression—the potential for a deeper self-understanding—there are also real dangers of misinterpreting its message. We do well to insist that any simple-minded approach to depression needs to be avoided.

Chapter 4

Breaking Through

> All breakdown is not pathological; some break-
> down is breakthrough.
> R. D. Laing, *The Divided Self* [1]

When the rites of passage have concluded, the "passen-
gers" have arrived at their destination. Clearly they are
adults. Having proven themselves worthy of being called
adults, they are now publicly acknowledged as full members
of the tribe. And the acknowledgment accorded the novices'
transformation into adults pertains to their transformation in
a comprehensive way,—spiritually, physically, sexually. No
tribal member has any doubts that those who have under-
gone this initiation can take their place alongside the other
adults in the tribal society.

The contrast between the novices' clear-cut achievement of adulthood, acknowledged by the tribal community,
and the inconclusive, unacknowledged breakthroughs of
people in transition today is striking. The breakthrough or
emergence from a transition is not clearly a breakthrough
unless there is some public acknowledgment.

But not even public acknowledgment is universally recognized within a contemporary society. While tribal societies
shared the same myths, belief systems, and worldview, modern pluralistic societies do not. We are far more complex,
and what might be recognized as a successful passage by
one segment goes unacknowledged by another. For example, answers to questions like, what does it mean to be a man

or a woman? vary depending on differing perspectives within the same culture. A soldier returning home from war is not automatically assumed to be mature spiritually because he has proven himself in battle. Nor is one thought to be mature simply because he is capable of fathering a child. Since modern societies are unable to arrive at a consensus on what it means for its members to be mature, different norms are established—getting a driver's license, being able to drink liquor, going into military service, getting married, being confirmed or bar mitzvahed, having one's first sexual experience, and various others.

The uncertainty of a breakthrough, resolution, or termination in contemporary transitions is both apparent in developmental transitions and problematic in persona identity transitions. When, for example, is a divorcing person really divorced? After the papers have been signed? When the partners physically separate, even though they might be still emotionally involved with one another? J. Randall Nichols suggests that couples go through a series of stages before they are finally divorced. He refers to them as five divorces, because no one of them conclusively ends the marriage.[2] But while one of the partners might have brought closure to the marriage, does that mean the other has as well? And who or what is necessary to acknowledge that the transition is over? Sometimes premature attempts to end transitions do not lead to genuine breakthroughs but to unhappy results. People who rush into second marriages to avoid the painful but necessary process of mourning the loss of the first marriage might find temporary relief but eventual disillusionment in the second.

Similarly, when does a widow or widower "get on" with life after the death of the spouse? What are the signs of a breakthrough or movement beyond simply being a widow or widower with a strong emotional connection to the deceased spouse? When does the person leave the cocoon of liminality? When is it time to stop grieving? Six months? A year after the spouse's death? Does a person wake up one day and say, "It's time to get on with my life! No more grieving!" Is there any person or group of people who will intervene at some point and recommend that the person resume a normal life? And what would a normal life be?

The absence of any supportive network that might assist us in times of transition becomes clear when we reflect on our need to be understood by others and find no one to grasp the meaning of what is happening to us. Consider the expression we use innumerable times daily as we try to make sense out of our lives. Repeatedly we ask, "Do you know what I mean?" as we attempt to communicate not only some idea—"Do you know *what* I mean?"—but more fundamentally, "Do you know what *I* mean?" that is, my meaning as a person. To ask what do *I* mean is to ask others (friends, lovers, neighbor, community) whether I make sense, have meaning, or count. For until the other says, "I know what *you* mean," that is, "I know your meaning," it isn't clear to me that I know what I mean to myself.

How we understand ourselves and make sense out of the events of our lives is partially dependent on a community that acknowledges and celebrates who we are and what we achieve. Not to mean is to be unacknowledged and unaffirmed. This is especially so with people who are going through transitions. Transition is transformation, the breaking up of one world and the breakthrough into another. But what can this mean to the person in transition if there is no one to whom or for whom this significant breakthrough means anything?

The point of this book is to identify aspects of contemporary transitions and to suggest how we might more effectively navigate them in a modern society. We already saw the

contrast between novices achieving status in primitive societies and the problems we encounter in contemporary transitions. Now we must identify those events that signify
breakthroughs as well as whatever events facilitate the transition from breaking away to breaking through. For even
though many struggle alone without any clear indication of
how or when they will complete their transitions, this doesn't
need to be the case.

The Breakthrough Is the Person

In a difficult transition the questions that arise are,
"When is this going to end? How much longer am I going to
feel this way? Is there anything I can do to get through this
more quickly?" Tempted as observers are to rush in and
offer consoling advice like, "There now, everything will be
fine! You'll see," they ought to resist.

One reason is that a breakthrough is not a destination
or goal external to us. It is what we are becoming. Breaking
through is a process in which the *person* is breaking up,
breaking down, and thereby breaking through. Questions
like, "How can I get through this faster?" and "When can I get
on with my life?" are unanswerable if the assumption is that
breaking through means arriving at some point in time when
everything is finally taken care of. These questions, understandably tinged with anguish, make little sense if breaking
through refers to some future date rather than to the process
of our transformation.

Seen as a process, in the initial phase of breaking up we
have already begun "coming out," or breaking through. Of
course, what is most obvious in the experience of breaking
up is the disturbance and upheaval of the status quo, not the
stirrings of a new outlook or direction. For example, breaking an unhealthy dependent relationship with a parent or
spouse is simultaneously the beginning of a breakthrough

towards self-reliance. Undeniably, this self-reliance is fragile for someone accustomed to relying heavily on another. Yet the anxiety doesn't negate the emergence (experienced as an emergency) into a new mode of being.

Another reason questions like, "When will it end? How long must I feel so lost and lonely?" cannot be easily answered has to do with the personality and concrete circumstances of the person in transition. For example, when is a parent reconciled to a son or daughter's leaving home? Fairly soon, if the parent has his or her own interests to pursue, but not so soon if the son or daughter has been the focal point of the parent's life. Moreover, if a child has been the only interest that husband and wife had in common, the transition might be even more difficult to complete.

When does someone get accustomed to retirement? This might depend on how many outside interests the person had before retiring or, if the person is married, what adjustments living at home with the spouse will require. One woman whose husband retired found herself locked in the bathroom muttering, "He has a right to retire! He has a right to retire! This is his house, too!" as he roamed the house offering suggestions how to manage her affairs. Or suppose that an unhappily married couple agree that divorce is the only resolution to their mutual animosity; this doesn't mean the divorce terminates the transition. Each of them might still be grieving years later over the pluses of their marriage.

Minibreakthroughs

Although questions like, "How much longer do we need to wait before completing a transition?" are difficult to answer, there are clues or signs as to whether or not we are achieving a breakthrough in our becoming. These signs we can designate "minibreakthroughs." These signs are not necessarily understood at the time as breakthroughs, nor do they necessarily feel pleasant or hopeful.

Thus, children who no longer want to go on family outings or vacations get very testy and whiny towards their parents. These are the minibreakthroughs or signs of a breakthrough from an embeddedness or identification with the "we" of the family. Adolescents who are naysayers, moody, and restless are showing signs of a more independent mode of living. They might also exhibit signs of resistance to growing up by resorting to childish behavior, for example, throwing spitballs in a classroom. Breaking through comes at a price for all involved.

Another minibreakthrough might be a growing awareness of our hitherto unacknowledged dependency needs—an emergence of the need to complement our receptive side with assertiveness, our serious side with playfulness, our guarded side with openness, even through behaviors that seem totally at odds with our personality. Thus, people who ordinarily say yes to every request that comes along find themselves beginning to say no and often feeling guilty about it. Or people who ordinarily are pillars of strength and very restrained break down in uncontrollable weeping. Another minibreakthrough that might initially manifest itself as a descent into complete relativism might be an ability to acknowledge and tolerate multiple perspectives without losing commitment to a perspective we had previously extolled as the only point of view.

Because these minibreakthroughs are signs of the fundamental breakthrough that the person is, we might be inclined to identify these signs as the *fundamental* breakthrough, because in some instances these signs are so vivid and memorable that they appear to summarize the whole transition. Such signs might be a revelatory dream, a chance encounter that appears to change our life, an apparently decisive moment. Yet the things that are so significant and memorable are part of the larger picture of transformation from breakup to breakdown. The snap decision of one in transition is often a minibreakthrough preceded by and followed by other moments in a whole process of decision making occurring on different levels of the personality.

One sign of a breakthrough that might seem completely contradictory is arriving at an impasse. An impasse is a dead-end. It occurs during a crisis in which we don't know which way to turn, which decision is correct. We might have only a few choices or many. Each situation has its advantages and disadvantages. Reasoning for or against any one is of no help. Indeed, it is the failure of reason and logic that has brought us to the impasse. In this situation we might look to others for help, but the impasse remains, even if bright, knowledgable counselors recommend one course of action over another. And the impasse continues precisely because everybody is resorting to what has so far not been helpful: reason and logic.

Reason's failure to resolve the impasse points to reason's limitations and the necessity of paying attention to the heart's desire. We might have reached a conclusion, *A,* that from a rational perspective is preferable to *B.* Yet we don't *feel* right about it, our heart is not in the decision. We understand why one choice is logically more commendable, but we cannot bring ourselves to make the more logical choice. What then should we do? Should we listen to our heart's desire or suppress it?

Moving between head and heart, we feel caught, suspended. "Hang in there," seems to be all that we can do. Yet there is wisdom in hanging in there. During a transition we want desperately to do something to effect a change. Yet we feel unable to do anything. Possibly the tension in hanging between wanting to do and feeling unable to do is the necessary condition for the breakthrough that we are becoming.

And when we finally experience a breakthrough, it isn't clear who did the doing. By this I mean that we wondered and wondered what to do, and then at some point we discover a decision has been made. The person is the breakthrough that has been moving (mysteriously, it seems) in a direction, and any decision the person makes confirms what has already happened in the person's life.

The active-passive nature of this breakthrough is reflected in Rilke's advice when he counsels,

> have patience with everything unsolved in your heart and try to love the questions themselves as if they were locked rooms or books written in a very foreign language. Don't search for the answers, which could not be given to you now, because you would not be able to live them. And the point is to live everything. Live the questions now. Perhaps then, some day far in the future, you will gradually, without even noticing it, live your way into the answer.[3]

"Living the questions" characterizes our actively engaging them, while "living into the answers without noticing" refers to the passive quality of what we are doing.

Just as some signs indicate a breakthrough, other signs point to a breakthrough being unlikely. Refusing to grieve when grieving is the appropriate response, as in a divorce or the death of a spouse or the loss of a job, are tell-tale signs that a person isn't even acknowledging the necessity of going through a transition. Similarly, an excessive rigidity and an unquestioned allegiance to the status quo indicate resistance to any kind of change.

Attempting to go through transitions too quickly so that one doesn't feel the pain of loss aborts the process. This refusal to "live" the transition means there can be no breaking through that is dependent on insight gained in experiencing the loss during the breakdown phase.

Holding Communities

Once more I find my inspiration from the work of Robert Kegan. In speaking about the kind of support necessary for people going through developmental transitions, Kegan refers to British psychiatrist W. D. Winnicott's expression, "the holding environment."[4] Winnicott was referring to the mother's function in relation to her small infant as one of holding the infant psychologically as well as physically. The environment, which is the mother herself, is the psychosocial container for the infant. That is, the mother and infant are so fused that the infant's self-experience is inseparable from the self's experience of the mother. When mother is distressed or anxious, the infant's self-experience is one of anxiety and distress. How the mother cares for her baby is what holding is all about. Feeding, soothing, and responding to the baby's needs, knowing when to hold and when to put the child down, fussing too much or too little, are all ways of holding the infant. So holding refers to the whole way of relating to the child.

Kegan extends the idea of the holding environment at infancy to include all the environments that hold people as they mature throughout the life cycle. He refers to these holding environments as "cultures of embeddedness."[5] Examples include the family, the school, and the marital community. How we are held as children, as adolescents, and as adults is crucial to how successfully we negotiate our developmental transitions. For Kegan, there are three functions that these holding environments or cultures perform: (1) they hold on through affirmation; (2) they let go through contradiction; (3) they remain in place through continuity, that is, they endure.

Exactly what these functions mean within the context of Kegan's work is not important here. Rather, we can adapt Kegan's ideas on the various holding environments to any kind of community that might hold people going through transitions. We can fruitfully explore the possibilities of holding communities by thinking of them as psychologically holding people in transition in the three ways already stated.

1. Holding communities hold on. As we begin to change or break away from the previous way of identifying ourselves (e.g., as a spouse whose husband or wife has now died or as someone recently divorced) we are bound to be disoriented, confused, lost. What we need are friends who hold on. They are with us in our confusion. They don't try to make us feel better, or say that things will get better, or tell us to think of all the good times to lessen the pain. No, they are with us as we feel the pain. They don't need to rush in with the Kleenex to stop our crying.

We can imagine a widow, for example, whose grief is compounded because she wasn't there when her husband died or who maybe feels remorseful because they hadn't gotten along as well as they could. Where are we in this? Do we try to fix things up? Mend things? Or are we willing to let it stand? Or when someone asks where God was when the person's mother died a horrible death? Do we feel we have to give an explanation, interpret what's happened, make the person feel good? What we need to do is simply hold the person by being there, offering a space in our lives for that person.

"Holding on" should be contrasted with "holding on to." "Holding on to" is an attempt to keep things as they were. It is resistance to change. "Well, before long you'll be back to your old self." Or "You'll see, time heals everything." Or if you've broken up with somebody, "Well, you'll find somebody else." But the truth is time doesn't heal everything. And things will never be the same. And we won't be our old selves again. Holding on *to* looks at the experiences of loss and feeling lost, of being confused, of getting anxious, as alien experiences that possess us. Holding on *to* obscures our view of these feelings as growing pains signaling the evolving, changing person we are in the present. Growing pains become more painful if we resist the pain or think it ought not to be there. They signal that life is a process of losing and finding ourselves. Do we know people to whom we can go, people who can hold us without holding on to us?

2. *Holding communities let go.* It is important that there be people in our lives who are on the side of us that needs to leave home, even when we don't want to acknowledge that need. "Home" is a metaphor, a way of speaking about the present arrangement, the way things currently are. "Leaving home" is a way of saying that it is time to move beyond the current arrangement. We are speaking about changes in self-understanding. The people in our lives who don't challenge us—who don't contradict our prevailing way of seeing and doing things—overhold us and consequently inhibit us from maturing. We need the help of those with whom we have identified and on whom we have depended in order to differentiate ourselves from them. Otherwise we pay the price of stifling conformity and covert anger or depression.

Letting go tests the community's capacity for opposition to otherness. By this I mean we who are friends of people who are changing are challenged to hold them even as they go through their own naysaying stage. Often transitions involve protests or repudiations of previous identifications—anger, hostility, disillusionment at the church, family, spouse, or work for holding one back. We might be inclined to moralize or lecture people who are at odds with previous alliances, especially if we ourselves are on the side of these alliances. (Think of people going through divorce who feel very hostile towards an ex-spouse or women who have experienced discrimination in the church.) The transition through which they are going is initially characterized by protest. And as we saw earlier, it is an attempt to establish one's separateness from that with which one has been identified.

3. *Holding communities endure.* If we want to achieve an identity as autonomous human beings, we need to leave home—meaning the people in our lives with whom we have been identified and on whom we have been dependent. Yet leaving home is only the first step in the journey. Repeatedly, we also need to return home to be integrated or reconciled as adults with many of the people we have left behind. It is important that there be those around who are ready to receive us. Is it asking too much that they be there or that we be there for people coming back home? In other words, are there people who stick around in our lives, who don't drop us because we are going through our changes? Are there people who are there after the divorce? After the death of a spouse? After we go through our upheavals? Our crises of faith? Our wild times? Are there people on the welcoming committee? "You're one of ours. You belong. We understand you had to leave but we want you to know we're still here for you." Is it being too idealistic to think that there should be people who remain in place for the homecoming? Let us hope not!

Support Groups

These questions invite us to consider the viability of the support group as a holding community for people in transition. The importance of support groups in this country cannot be underestimated. According to Robert Wuthnow in his book *Sharing the Journey: Support Groups and America's New Quest for Community,* 40 percent of the adult population claim to be involved in "a small group that meets regularly and provides caring and support for those who participate in it." In other words, approximately 75 million adult

Americans are meeting regularly for some kind of small group interaction and support. This figure does not include all the groups children and teenagers attend.

The emergence of so many support groups is a response to people's need for community, as the subtitle to Wuthnow's book suggests. And this need for community is itself a response

> both to the intense yearning for the sacred that characterizes the American people and to the breakdown of communities, neighborhoods, families, and other sources of personal support....The fragmented lives that many of us lead provide an *incentive* to seek community in support groups. But the religious traditions that are so much a part of American culture legitimate this quest by telling us that community is important, and, indeed, by leading us to believe that community is also the way to find spirituality and transcendence.[6]

Support groups come in all shapes, colors, and sizes and can be found to meet virtually everyone's taste. There are support groups that are deeply rooted in religious traditions and appeal to persons from those traditions (e.g., bible study, prayer fellowship). There are special-interest groups that work on special projects, (e.g., discussing social or political issues, helping people in their communities, engaging in sports or hobbies together). There are self-help groups that generally provide mutual aid or mutual support to their members. These are composed of peers who share common experiences or situations; they are run by and for their members and operate on a voluntary, nonprofit basis. Among these groups are Alcoholics Anonymous, Al-Anon (family members of alcoholics), Narcotics Anonymous, Overeaters Anonymous, and Co-Dependents Anonymous (for people who compulsively take responsibility for others: widows, the divorced, workaholics, etc.).

His observations on the variety, function, and value of small groups help us to determine whether they might be considered "holding communities," as we have described them. What clearly emerges from Wuthnow's study is that these support groups generally affirm their members.

> Small groups allow people to know one another at a more intimate level. They provide contexts in which doubts and fears, personal aims and aspirations, grief, joy, and the minor victories of everyday life can be shared. They function well because they provide at least some of the intimacy that families and friendships and neighborhoods have provided. They draw people out of themselves and help round out their personalities.[7]

While Wuthnow generally praises the existence and great variety of support groups in which the members are able to discuss their problems and affirm one another, he does point out that the potential danger of the movement stems from this variety.

> If we can find a group that fits perfectly with our individual needs at the moment, then we may not be challenged by that group to become anything different from what we might be anyway, we may move on to another group when our interests change, and we may find it difficult to stay with other commitments that demand more of us.[8]

Not only might a support group not be challenging, it might hold on to members by resisting any change among those who are beginning to question ideas, attitudes, beliefs, and behaviors that have governed or guided the group in their meetings. Subtle pressures "to do as we do or else" might keep the members in line, but pressure, however subtle, is still pressure. Unfortunately, there always will be persons alone or collectively manipulating others to accept things the way they are as the way they ought to be.

In such cases it isn't clear how willing these persons are to stick around when any member of the group becomes oppositional, as often happens with people in transition. It takes real commitment not only to affirm but to stay with someone who is going through a difficult, lengthy transition. Understandably, the members of support groups are in these groups to receive as well as to give affirmation. How long the members will be supportive of someone going through a painful and protracted transition before they decide to withdraw from the group is a good question.

Of the different kinds of support groups, self-help groups seem most likely to challenge as well as affirm. As stated earlier, members assist one another in working through problems they have in common. Whether the problem is some form of addiction, codependency, loss, or the like, the members are already immersed in liminality. They share the same wounds and so are in a position to appreciate each other's pain and what is needed to alleviate that pain. People going through a divorce, for example, already come into the group with a depth of understanding. This inspires them to commit themselves to one another's well-being because a commitment to help others is at the same time a way of working through their own similar problems. Yet whatever the issue, members of support groups benefit from listening to others' stories and by sharing their own struggles. As they help clarify and challenge others' motives and defenses, their own issues are clarified and challenged as well.

There is also something about self-help groups that seems to approximate Victor Turner's notion of *communitas* in transitions.[9] Recall that Turner indicated that in rites of passage, those undergoing the rites were ritually nonpersons, they were temporarily stripped of identity. In order to be re-created or reborn as adults, they had to go through a "ritual humiliation"—reduced to nothing so that they could be molded or formed into adults by the tribal elders. The status and roles that had distinguished them from one another in their tribal society prior to the ritual meant nothing in the rites of passage. All that they shared was a common humanity. Bound together in a common journey towards adult status, they shared experiences they never had and never would share with any other members of the tribe. Once the ritual was over and they had returned to their tribal society, the memories of what they had shared would be with them until they died.

Something of *communitas* emerges in self-help groups, especially in twelve-step programs. For example, at AA meetings people introduce themselves, not by giving the credentials that distinguish them in their social, political, or domestic lives; rather, they give only their first names. "Hello, I'm Mary." Stripped of whatever had given them a sense of importance by the crises that brought them down, they come together to share with one another their stories, not for the purpose of playing the game of one-upmanship but for admitting that they have hit rock bottom and are in need of help. In sharing this admission, they shared an affinity with one another that spouses, relatives, and friends, however close, could not share. Their experience of bonding can be so profound that many people in these groups identify their religious experiences with the group rather than with a religious institution.

We get some sense of this bonding if we recall being temporarily stranded in an airport or a shelter for earthquake or flood victims. In these instances the impact people have on one another has nothing to do with status but with their being "in it together." Compassion, or suffering *with* others because they are in the same predicament, generates instances of *communitas* that are long remembered after the crisis has passed. These are the times when we find ourselves confiding to strangers something of ourselves we wouldn't dream of telling the people closest to us!

By way of summary, we might say that support groups are able to function as holding communities in limited ways. This is not meant to disparage their importance. Their popularity argues their necessity. As Wuthnow has pointed out, there is a problem in the breakdown of the traditional holding communities, and support groups are a limited response to that problem.

"Limited" here simply means that these support groups are not with people for the long haul. Members affirm, challenge, and even commit themselves to one another's well-being, but none of the support groups have been part of each other's personal histories. It is this "sticking with" the person through one's leaving home and returning home, through losing and finding oneself, through one's opposition to and acceptance of the community, that a support group cannot provide its members.

However, our awareness of the importance of a holding community alerts us to the fact that we cannot achieve a breakthrough on our own. We are dependent throughout our lives on supportive communities affirming, challenging, and being an enduring presence. Yet traditional holding communities (family, friends, neighbors, etc.) are not always available, and so we look for alternatives. The proliferation of support groups responds to the need for community. But there are limits to how adequately they meet the criteria of holding communities.

Part Two

The Ultimate Breaks

We have looked primarily although not exclusively through the lenses of psychology and anthropology to interpret transitional experiences of breaking up, down, and through. These perspectives have yielded interesting insights into our ordinary experiences. While we didn't explicitly treat matters of ultimacy, we did so implicitly. Now is the time to address ultimacy explicitly. But what do we mean by the ultimate, and what is our intention in addressing it explicitly?

"Ultimacy" refers to whatever or whoever God is for us *operatively,* that is, whoever commands our attention, gives direction, and centers our lives. Ideally, what we profess and what we actually live would correspond with each other. But often this isn't the case. What we profess isn't necessarily what governs our lives, although what is operative need not be at odds with what we profess. For example, we might identify ourselves as an atheist or agnostic but conduct ourselves as an ideal Christian or Jew. Conversely, we might define ourselves as Christian yet behave otherwise.

Here we will deal explicitly with matters of ultimacy. Recalling that the word *implicit* derives from the Latin *implicare,* which means "to fold in," the observations in the previous chapters on breaking up, down, and through had ultimate concerns folded into them. For example, we noted that setups and letdowns could only be explained by our need for meaning, but we did not draw out the ultimate implications of what this meaning might be. Nor did we explore the ultimate implications of loss when we considered what we lose in our letdowns. We referred often to chaotic and confusing changes in how we understand ourselves and our world. But we left unexplored how we might understand chaos beyond its being an interruption on the level of interpersonal relationships. While limited references to rites of passage suggested that our transitions might be potentially transformative, we had not gotten much beyond hinting at their spiritual significance.

Why be explicit about the ultimate? Because what is left implicit can easily go unrecognized and might therefore be lost. By becoming consciously aware of the transcendent dimension in our ordinary experiences of breaking up, down, and through, we can celebrate what is of ultimate significance in what might have struck us as being at best disruptive and at worst destructive in our lives. When we view our experiences through the spiritual lens, we discover that it is as impossible to avoid matters of transcendence in the discussion of transitions as it is to avoid breathing and continue to live. Even if we might never consciously advert to the ultimate, even if we desire to ignore, forget, or denigrate it, we deceive ourselves if we think it is possible to exist without this concern.

I hope that in what follows we shall become more aware of the transcendent breaking into our lives during transitions. Enhanced awareness enables us to celebrate these times by viewing the ordinary in an extraordinary way. For many of us it might be consoling to realize we are being sustained on our journey by more than our own efforts.

In the next chapter, *Addictions as the Search for God,* we return to the subject of setups and letdowns, this time with a view towards understanding setups as the idols we inevitably construct in our search for ultimacy. Confronting our idols ushers us into the experience of the dark night implicit in breaking up, down, and through.

In the last chapter, *The Attitude Is Contemplative,* we shall look at the cultural barriers that obscure what is happening to us in our transitions. As we proceed, it shall become clearer that what we really need to develop is a contemplative attitude towards them. Finally, we shall consider how to become more contemplative in our transitions.

Chapter 5

Addictions
as the Search
for God

People who talk to us about our idols usually scold us for making them. They are quick to scold us for relying on what is ultimately unreliable, for making absolute what is not absolute, for treating as ultimately true what is not ultimately true, and therefore false. But that judgment is so easy to make as to be glib. That our idols are futile and crumbling, that we are not finally saved by them, that we are trapped in bondage to them—all this is well known by any of us much beyond the age of trusting in leaves and snowmen and kites. The most shrill scolding doesn't tell us as much as the grief we already know. Instead, let us rescue our hopes from the scolding and the grief, and let us celebrate idol making, for our idols testify to our persistent hope, our long-range trust and our capacities for urgent commitments.

James Dittes, *The Male Predicament*[1]

Is it possible that the idols we create are not necessarily the evil that preachers would have us believe? Would it be outrageous to suggest that idol making has a pedagogical value in assisting us to discover what is of ultimate importance? Or that without our idols we might never come to appreciate transcendent presence? We can answer these questions by reviewing and deepening our understanding of the importance of setups and letdowns. This review will enable us to focus on the role of the dark night in our experiences of breaking up, down, and through.

Recalling that the object of enchantment is what promises (or what we *believe* promises) fulfillment, we can understand addictions as various forms of enchantment that always promise more than they can deliver. As in romantic love we look to the beloved to center us and invest him or her with our center, our self, so it is in the relationship between addicts and their object of desire. And just as we idealize in instances of falling in love, we also idealize in the process of becoming addicted. We invest work or alcohol or drugs or food with godlike qualities that fascinate and hold our attention as if it were god.

St. Augustine's comment that our hearts are restless until they rest in God is most appropriate here. The heart seeks to rest in whatever seems to offer the possibility of total fulfillment, and in return the heart invests the object of its hope with infinite value. It is true that some people are more vulnerable than others to becoming addicted. Circumstances (e.g., low self-esteem, stress, possible physiological predispositions to addiction) can accelerate the addictive process. However, a case for the inevitability of addiction in everyone's life can easily be made if we understand the urgency of the human heart to satisfy its longing and consequently its vulnerability to being captivated by whatever or whoever it perceives to promise that satisfaction.

We can go even further and state not only that is addiction inevitable but that forms of addiction awaken the desire for God. There are two reasons why this is so. First, we discover our passion for fulfillment in being drawn outside of ourselves by the object of enchantment. Second, in and through this enchantment we also discover qualities we have been taught to attribute to God alone: the power to center us, the be-all and end-all of life, the meaning of our existence. However, so mesmerized are we by the object of enchantment that we don't realize it is at best a pale imitation of what it promises to be. Addictions are not *Reality*. Still, they have served a purpose if they have awakened the heart's passion for total fulfillment but later frustrated the heart's desire by revealing their inability to be Reality.

James Dittes makes the same point about the heart's infinite longing and its inevitable frustration in attempting to find that fulfillment in any created reality. He says that our hope is based on a glimpse and on a withholding. Our hope is to be saved. And the form of this saving comes from our dreams, fantasies, stories told us, reconstructions of what other people's lives might be like, embellished memories—all giving us hints or foretastes of a state of sublime well-being. Of course, the products of our hope are our idols, which we expect will save us. Food, drugs, romantic involvements are potentially addictive and therefore potentially salvation for us. They become our saviors. But the glimpse of saving is only a glimpse and is threatened or withheld as soon as it is given. "Our yearning which is both the vision and the grief, both the glimpse and the withholding is all one move of aspiration: we reach, unable to grasp, just as what we grasp is not what we reach for. Saving must come from a distance."[2]

Wisdom of the Elder

This dual function of the object as setup in promising total fulfillment and as letdown in failing to deliver corresponds to certain religious rites of passage. Sam Gill, in an extremely perceptive article on rites of passage among some preliterate tribal societies, has shown that the goal of spiritual transformation in the novices or beginners is accomplished through a series of ceremonies in which enchantment and disenchantment play central roles.[3] In one initiation ceremony the elders of the community dress up as the tribal gods and present themselves as such to the wide-eyed novices. In another ceremony, although the elders again come disguised as the gods, they later reveal themselves not to be gods at all but the tribal elders. A sense of betrayal arises among the novices when they realize they have been duped.

Why are the novices encouraged to believe the gods are among them and then disabused of that very belief? According to Gill, there is an important pedagogical value in this. First, the novices are given the opportunity to experience the gods concretely and visibly in the masked elders parading as gods. The invisible becomes tangible and available. The gods can be located in space and time via the masked elders.

However, later the novices are discouraged from simply *identifying* the masked figures with the gods. The young novices are forced to realize that while the invisible becomes apparent in the visible, the invisible is always more than any of its appearances. In other words, the novices must arrive at a more sophisticated appreciation of the sacred and live with the realization that the sacred is here in this object, place, and thing but also that it exists beyond any of its concrete manifestations.

The objects of our fascinations or addictions are leads, clues, intimations, and partial disclosures of the Real. As such they are good. If we are ever to get started on the spiritual journey, it seems that we need to get "hooked" or fascinated by one or more of these objects as if they were complete Reality, just as the novices were taken in by the masked elders. And in our passionate drive toward this union, time and again we light on this person or that thing with the unspoken, perhaps unconscious assumption: This is it! This is what I am looking for! Without realizing it, we are setting ourselves up. We are expecting to find our total fulfillment in this or that limited reality.

We crave what we can touch, see, taste, hear. Addictive objects offer this. But like novices in primitive rites, we also need to experience disenchantment with our addictions. Letdown is inevitable when we discover the concrete other is not and can never be the All. It is not Reality. And our disillusionment or feeling of betrayal liberates us from viewing them as such. The point is, our being "illusioned" or hooked is as much a part of our spiritual journey in the search for Reality as is our being disillusioned.

Hooked on God

But couldn't we bypass all these addictions, these imitations of God, and search for God directly? Why settle for anything less than that which alone can satisfy the longing for total fulfillment? Yet the most subtle addiction is the god addiction. As with all other setups and illusions, addiction to God means we have certain expectations, assumptions, and needs that help shape how God (or whatever name we give the Real) is to satisfy our longing. God must be male or female, white or black. God is the one who will deliver us from suffering, comfort us if we pray hard enough, and never abandon us. God will never abandon us. Just as we place demands on how a lover, friend, spouse, or business associate ought to relate to us, so we do on God. God is to be the glue that holds us together, the center of our lives—but the center as *we* need the center to be. This is a setup.

And the letdown? We pray and believe that God will heal a loved one, but the loved one dies in agony. We reflect on the holocaust or the mass murders in Russia, Cambodia, Yugoslavia, and we wonder what happened to the "just" God. God seems more enemy than friend. And our disillusionment with God gives rise to what the great spiritual teachers refer to as the experience of the dark night.

In the Dark About God

When we speak of being in the dark, we mean that we haven't a clue as to what someone is talking or thinking about. We are at an impasse, dead-ended. The dark night is our being in the dark about God. We have no idea who God is anymore, and we've arrived at an impasse in our relationship. From time to time we experience similar impasses in our relationship with friends or spouses. We think we know one another, and one day we argue, discover something unsettling about ourselves and the other, and reach an impasse in our relationship. Maybe the impasse lasts for days or months. During this time, while we are in the dark, we might begin to realize how we have misinterpreted, distorted, and misunderstood one another based on our needs and expectations.

The spiritual giants also tell us that we need to remain in the dark, that is, in the dark night. There we need to be purified of misconceptions and distortions of who and what this Reality is. In other words, we need to get beyond our illusions about God.

The stripping of illusions is a struggle because we are comfortable with the images and ideas of God that have guided us for years in relating to God, ourselves, and others. The anticipation of losing the meaning these images and their attendant belief systems have afforded provokes anxiety and in certain instances intensifies resistance to any change whatsoever. Resistance to change leads to placing undue emphasis on mastering the "essentials," memorizing formulae, insisting on conformity, and appealing to an authority to ensure that no change occurs at all. Underlying this resistance is the perceived threat to individual and group identity. If we were to give up certain ways of thinking about God, then who would we be?

What isn't understood or appreciated is that the point of the dark night is not the *destruction* but the *relativization* of images or ideas about God. In other words, in our spiritual journey we need to be reminded that no set of images or ideas, no doctrinal formulae, no dogmatic decisions can adequately describe or articulate who or what God is. We cannot stop at any wayside shrine and think our pilgrimage is at an end. We need a healthy tension between recognizing the value as well as the limits of our images and ideological formulations about God. The reality of God is mediated through the image. But no image is to be identified exclusively with God. Any time we identify ideas, images, or formulae with Reality, we are like foolish people who confuse the recipe for chocolate cake with the cake! A recipe is invaluable in giving us a way to experiencing the cake, but it's hardly a substitute.

Given our longing to pin down the object of our longing, such partial identifications seem inevitable. The Hindu scriptures, the Upanishads, speak of the ultimate reality as "asti, asti" and "neti, neti." "Asti, asti" means God is this and God is that. We can discover God in everything! On the other hand, God is also neti, neti. God is not this and God is not that. *No* concrete reality *is* God. Every thing mirrors God but no thing is God. Disillusionment in the dark night is the painful but fruitful realization of this truth.

In a similar vein the great German mystic Meister Eckhart writes of the breakthrough born of our desire for union with the Godhead, the God without a name, when we move beyond our created images.

> The intellect can never find rest. It aspires to God not as he is the Holy Spirit or as he is the Son: it flees from the Son. Nor does it want God inasmuch

as he is God. Why? Because, as such, he still carries a name. And even if there were a thousand gods, it would still break beyond: it wants him where he has no name. It wants something more noble, something better than God as having a name. What then does the intellect want? it does not know; it wants him as he is the Father. This is why Saint Philip says: "Lord, show us the Father and it is enough for us." It wants him as he is the marrow out of which goodness springs; it wants him as he is the nucleus from which goodness flows; it wants him as he is the root, the vein, from which goodness exudes. Only there is he the Father.[4]

Alan Watts once suggested that we get together annually and burn the bible. He was not being disrespectful. On the contrary, he recognized the importance of scriptures. But he also realized that the bible isn't God and we ought not to confuse the important but limited expressions of God with the living God. A ritual bible burning might help us to be mindful of this truth.

But there is more to address in a transition toward ultimacy than disillusionment. Along with disillusionment there is very often depression. That too is part of the dark night. Here it is not simply a matter of being in the dark but of feeling that darkness as a heavy weight on one's soul.

Ultimacy in Developmental Changes

Recall that Kegan relates depression to these developmental changes in which we lose our ability to make sense of ourselves and our world. This loss has spiritual significance because it is about understanding ourselves and our world in an "ultimate" way. Depression arises in the process of "taking for ultimate what is only preliminary, the making of any given way of knowing the world, the way of knowing."[5] Defending one particular way of understanding ourselves and our world, we end up idolizing it. It is Reality for us! And when we begin to go through a transition (e.g., from the socializing self to the self-authorizing self), we are neither ourselves nor any longer at home in our world. Confronted with our now inappropriate way of putting together our world, we feel inadequate. As our world is breaking down, what appears through the cracks is frightening, not because of what is there, but because of what *isn't* there. It is the Void, the apparent absence of meaning.

Depression becomes spiritually significant not only because it signifies the loss of our ability to interpret life from what we perceive to be a limited perspective but precisely because it is the Void that reveals the limitations of our former point of view. In revealing its limits, the Void discloses our former perspective for what it is: a form of idolatry. The familiar, certain way in which we conduct our lives—the truth as we see it and insist on seeing it—loses its familiarity and certainty against the horizon of this emptiness. Yet in revealing the current limits of our knowing, the Void also reveals the possibility of knowing in a new way.

Kegan relies on H. Richard Niebuhr's use of the word *Void* as he attempts to show this spiritual dimension of developmental transitions—the movement from the loss of making meaning to the creation of new meaning. He refers approvingly to Niebuhr's description of the experience of the Void as the transition from God the Enemy to God the Friend. What was at first experienced as hostile and inimical is later experienced as friendly.[6] Since our experience of God is mediated through our current way of understanding the truth of ourselves and our world, God is our trustworthy friend in a familiar world. But when the world becomes a threatening place to live because it no longer makes sense, then God is mediated as God the Enemy—until a new world of meaning emerges. Then God becomes the Friend again.

This process of revealing the inadequacy of any current understanding of ourselves and our world in taking as ultimate what is preliminary—a truth as *the* Truth—might remind us of the tribal rites which Sam Gill described in his article on disenchantment. The novices are led to believe that the gods *are* their manifestation but then are disillusioned of this "truth" in order to know the Real in a new way.

For a better understanding of the Void, we might look to the theologian Urban Holme's reflection on the meaning of the liminal as antistructure, that which is beyond definition or classification and is therefore unlimited.

> As one moves over the limits of society into the antistructure, one becomes aware of that which is without limit, the boundless. He is confronted by infinite being, which is ultimately the divine itself; but he is confronted with it, not as meaning or something to be known, but rather as a hidden meaning or something that is not known. He reaches out beyond the horizons of his ordered knowing. It is chaos, or experience not reduced to meaning, not ordered.[7]

The liminal is the unlimited, infinite, divine not revealed as something known. Chaos confronts us, the void. However, for Holmes this chaos is not an empty space but

> a pregnant void. Chaos has no form and no order; it is pure potentiality from which the dynamic of life springs into our consciousness. It is the waters of life. From the abyss of chaos emerges that to which God gives shape through us, and which we call the created order. Chaos is the precondition

and the source of power for life in its various degrees of structured existence.[8]

What is initially experienced as something not known, as hidden meaning, is now experienced as the source of life. For Kegan, too, the Void, initially experienced as threatening, is revealed as our friend as we move through the transition from meaning destroyed to meaning re-created.

Depression and disillusionment go hand in hand in the experience of the dark night as we become purified of illusions as to what is worthy of worship and what is idolatrous. Whether any actual thought of God occurs as people attempt to clarify what they are going through is an open question. Many of us don't think of ourselves as being spiritual or religious. Consequently, we don't describe experiences from this frame of reference. Yet even we who do identify ourselves as spiritual might never reflect on these experiences in spiritual terms, or if we do, we reflect on them negatively, as loss of faith. Many of us do not interpret depression and disillusionment as harbingers of a change in understanding ourselves and our world. Nor do we see these dark visitors as beckoning us to the necessary purification of what is worthy of our yearning for the ultimate.

Kegan's description of transitional phenomena as the breakup of what has given meaning to life and the emergence of a new way of knowing finds resonance in Evelyn Underhill's description of the dark night:

> The self, in its necessary movement towards higher levels of reality, loses and leaves behind certain elements of its world long loved but now outgrown....The self is being pushed into a new world where it does not feel at home, but has not yet reached the point at which it enters into conscious possession of its second or adult life.

Psychologically, then, the "Dark Night of the Soul" is due to the double fact of the exhaustion of an old state, and the growth towards a new state of consciousness. It is a "growing pain" in the organic process of the self's attainment of the Absolute.[9]

Underhill's description of the dark night accords well with Kegan's ideas of the change in making meaning as she writes of the change in consciousness from one level towards another—"the attainment of the Absolute." We resist being pushed into a new world that doesn't feel like home. The Absolute must seem like the enemy rather than the soul's fulfillment. Yet the Absolute *is* the soul's fulfillment, *its* true friend and lover. In transitions we might be moving towards greener pastures, but for many that vision is obscured because of the dark night emerging from the breakdown of the known world. But the dark night is itself vision, because we see by virtue of what isn't there the limits, illusions, and inadequacies of what we had regarded as ultimate. Qoheleth's cry, "Vanity of vanities! All is vanity" (Eccl 1:2) is not a cry of despair but the dark insight that what we take to be substantial is ultimately empty of meaning if we idolize it.

Tolstoy's Dark Night

A striking example of the experience of the dark night is to be found in Leo Tolstoy's *Confessions*. At about the age of fifty, Tolstoy began to have moments of perplexity, as if he didn't know how to live or what to do. Life had been enchanting, but it became flat, sober, dead. Things that had held meaning were now meaningless. More and more he asked the questions, "Why?" and "What does it all lead to?" At first, he thought that if he took the time, he would be able to answer these questions. But the questions became more insistent, and what he thought would pass now would not leave him.

> I felt that something had broken within me on which my life had always rested, that I had nothing left to hold on to, and that morally my life had stopped. An invincible force impelled me to get rid of my existence, in one way or another....It was a force like my old aspiration to live, only it impelled me in the opposite direction. It was an aspiration of my whole being to get out of life. All this took place at a time when so far as all my outer circumstances went, I ought to have been completely happy.[10]

Tolstoy asks himself whether there is any purpose in life that the death that awaits him doesn't undo or destroy. He wonders why he should live at all. While suicide was naturally the consistent course dictated by his intellect, Tolstoy writes:

> Yet whilst my intellect was working, something else in me was working too, and kept me from the deed—a consciousness of life, as I may call it, which was like a force that obliged my mind to fix itself in another direction and draw me out of my situation of despair....I can call this by no other name than that of a thirst for God. This craving for God had nothing to do with the movement of my ideas—in fact, it was the direct contrary of that movement—but it came from my heart.[11]

William James comments that what is of interest was Tolstoy's absolute

> disenchantment with ordinary life, and the fact that the whole range of habitual values may, to a man

as full of faculty as he was, come to appear so ghastly a mockery. When disillusionment has gone as far as this, there is seldom a *restitutio ad integrum*. One has tasted of the fruit of the tree, and the happiness of Eden never comes again....The process is one of redemption, not of mere reversion to natural health, and the sufferer, when saved, is saved by what seems to him a second birth, a deeper kind of conscious being than he could enjoy before.[12]

James's observations about not being able to return to one's former way of living—"a reversion to natural health"—and "saved by...a second birth, a deeper kind of conscious being" echo Underhill's insights into the transition from one kind of consciousness to another.

Tolstoy's transition took a couple of years as he gradually came to believe in the infinite as the common people did. Then life grew possible. During this two-year period he came to the conviction that his trouble hadn't been with life in general but with a life of artificiality and personal ambition. He needed to change. And one day a breakthrough occurred.

I remember one day in early spring, I was alone in the forest, lending my ear to its mysterious noises. I listened, and my thought went back to what for these three years it always was busy with—the quest of God. But the idea of him, I said, how did I ever come by the idea?

And again there arose in me, with this thought, glad aspirations towards life. Everything in me awoke and received a meaning....Why do I look farther? a voice within me asked. He is there: he, without whom one cannot live. To acknowledge God and to live are one and the same thing.

God is what life is. Well, then! live, seek God, and there will be no life without him.[13]

James remarks, "His crisis was the getting of his soul in order, the discovery of its genuine habitat and vocation, the escape from falsehoods into what for him were ways of truth. It was a case of heterogeneous personality tardily and slowly finding its unity and level."[14]

Tolstoy's account of his dark night reminds us that the dangers of this journey ought not to be underestimated. In depression we might interpret what we are going through as a call to commit suicide. If the loss of meaning or the inability to make sense out of life leads us to the conclusion that life is pointless, suicide might seem to be the only viable option. If it is a perspective on life, a way of understanding ourselves and our world that needs to die, then it would be a tragic mistake to interpret depression as meaning life is pointless. The distinction that David Rosen makes between egocide and suicide is crucial in experiences like Tolstoy's.

What we have learned from our reflections on the spiritual dimension of disillusionment and depression teaches that transitions can be occasions for spiritual transformation or conversion experiences. Through these conversions we become aware of the idols we have constructed and the progressive realization of their inability to be the Truth or the Real for us. We become disillusioned and depressed because of this growing realization. But out of these "negative" experiences it is possible to emerge with an expanded awareness of who we are in relation to the Other (e.g., The world, others, God). This expansion of awareness means seeing more distinctly what is self and what is Other, as opposed to seeing ourselves and the Other in a more limited and limiting way.

This seeing initially takes place in a dark night, which is

the purification of our illusions regarding what is self and what is Other, that is, what we see and what we have needed to see in our projections onto the Other. Although God appears to be the Enemy in these dark nights, as new meaning emerges, God might reappear as Friend.

Chapter 6

The Attitude
Is Contemplative

> I've stopped thinking all the time of what happened
> yesterday. And stopped asking myself what's going
> to happen tomorrow. What's happening today, this
> minute? That's what I care about. I say: What are
> you doing at this moment, Zorba? 'I'm sleeping.'
> Well, sleep well. What are you doing at this
> moment, Zorba? 'I'm kissing a woman.' Well, kiss
> her well, Zorba, and forget all the rest while you're
> doing it; there's nothing else, only you and her.
>
> Nikos Kazantzakis, *Zorba the Greek*[1]

Paradoxically, a transition can usher in a change so profound that dimensions of it might go completely unnoticed or unattended. Some of the reasons for this might
derive solely from our personal histories and psychological
dynamics such as an inability for self-reflection, external distractions at home or work, age at the time of transition, and
resistance to change. Other reasons might pertain to a mix-
ture of the personal and cultural factors. Our attitudes
towards what and how we notice are considerably shaped by
the culture in which we live. Most important of all, the attitude we develop toward transitions themselves will determine
whether we tend our transitions or not.

The attitude that we develop will enable us to be more
aware and available to the life within and around us. We can

call this a contemplative attitude. We foster this attitude of heightened awareness through the practice of being fully alive to the present moment. A consideration of the cultural attitudes that militate against contemplation will help us understand more clearly what being contemplative entails. What are these obstructing attitudes?

Barriers to Contemplation

Our Future Orientation to Reality. The first question we can ask ourselves is, are we in touch with the here and now, or are we always ahead of ourselves in an ever-receding future? To answer this question, all that we need to do is think about where we find ourselves mentally during the course of a day, a week, a month, a year. For example, when we sit down to eat breakfast, do we savor the food? Or are we simultaneously eating, reading the newspaper, and thinking about what we are going to have for lunch? If so, then we are not fully engaged in eating or reading or planning the menu. When we arrive at work, are we present to the person with whom we have an appointment? Or are we thinking of a later appointment with someone else? And when we are with the later appointment, are we now back mentally with our first appointment?

As our days go, so do our years. When we are in high school, we are looking forward to graduation. When we are in college, we are looking ahead to the job that will make our life worthwhile. When we finally get the job, we are more interested in a future promotion than anything else. After all, life is really worth living when the big bucks come in! Of course, everybody knows that it's not the job or the promotion but the thought of retirement that keeps us going! We look forward to that magical moment when we will be going to Sun City! Finally we get to Sun City—and two days later we get cardiac arrest and it's all over. So much for looking ahead!

What we miss and obviously have failed to treasure are the in-between times where our lives are really lived. In between what? In between the ever-receding magical moments when we think everything wonderful will happen— paradise regained! Yet it is in the in-between times that relatives, friends, strangers, and we ourselves may be anxious, sad, lonely, tense, angry, and depressed, and we never notice what is happening *now* because we are preoccupied with what will happen then. It is no secret that many marriages end because the partners have failed to notice in one another changes in moods, attitudes, and ideas over the years due to their preoccupation with anything but the present moment.

So powerful is this future orientation that the devaluation of the present moment enters into religion as well. Doing good is encouraged and avoiding evil discouraged by well-intentioned clergy because of a future reward or punishment. Present experiences are considered meaningful only to the extent that they are related to the future. Their value is external to the action themselves.

Our Need to Control the Direction of the Future. The need to control is often disguised under the admirable injunction, Be prepared. Similar common sense expressions are Pay attention! Don't get caught with your pants down! Look smart! Keep your eyes on the road! Stop daydreaming! Take notes! Plan ahead! Watch out for the guy next to you! People who embody this wisdom are alert and sharp as tacks. They don't trust just anybody and never let things pass them by. They have eyes in the back of their heads and never miss a trick.

Admirable as it is, if an approach to life cloaks our need to control the future, then it actually keeps us from living the full range of experiences, including our transitions. For if we need to be so controlling, nothing is left to chance. We don't want surprises, uninvited guests, upheavals, last-minute notices, being caught off guard. We are fearful that if we aren't prepared, if we aren't in control, we will be destroyed, overwhelmed by what lies in store. Our preparation then turns into paranoia, a fear of what we can't control—the unpredictable!

But the unpredictable does happen. Life is full of surprises—and the uncontrollable. Life is frequently messy, muddy, murky. Attempts to reduce life to the manipulable are not only futile, they also take the joy out of life. For it is in those moments when we lose control and surrender ourselves that we are filled with awe and joy. We lose our breath at the sight of a beautiful sunset; we are taken up by someone's unexpected thoughtfulness; we are overwhelmed with gratitude at kindnesses bestowed. Ecstasy is losing ourselves and finding ourselves in communion with something larger than ourselves.

It is only when we are willing to surrender ourselves to whatever is happening that we are really prepared. Preparation is availability to the predictable and the unpredictable. Good preparation is the willingness to be surprised rather than the willfulness to control and do away with all surprise. If we are too controlling, we shall miss out on the thousand and one ways life comes to us.

Our Pragmatic Orientation. Pragmatists value people and things in terms of their use. Waiters are valuable to the extent that they wait on tables. Dentists are valuable insofar as they do dentistry. An apple is valuable as food to be eaten. Business partners are valuable if they help our business. Movies are valuable if we "get something" out of them. Experiences are valuable if they are productive, lead somewhere, accomplish or achieve something. What a person or thing is apart from its use is irrelevant to the pragmatist.

Thus, the texture, shape, and variety of shadings in an apple are of no interest to someone who simply wants to satisfy his hunger. The shape, size, design of a chair are unimportant to someone whose sole concern is to satisfy the need to sit. A waiter's personal history never crosses a customer's mind as he calls for another cup of coffee. Even our intimate relationships can subtly turn into relationships that are functional. Think of spouses who complain bitterly of being treated as simply the breadwinner or housekeeper in the family.

A pragmatic orientation invariably means we see, hear, touch, and taste only in terms of our needs. We remain unaware of much of what is happening inside and outside of ourselves as long as we are committed to a pragmatic approach to people and things. We become habituated to noticing only what we need to notice and equally habituated to ignoring what we don't need.

This orientation works against us in times of transition. For if there were ever a need to be aware and available to dimensions of experience we have previously ignored, that need comes in times of change. Breakthroughs are more likely to occur when we begin to pay attention to what we had previously ignored because we had thought it unimportant or useless. Daydreams, intuitions, hunches, physical and emotional reactions, depression, fantasies, anxieties, fears we hadn't needed to notice are often the occasion for self-discoveries and breakthroughs into new levels of awareness.

One young man who saw himself as his mother's good son and subsequently tried to be good to everyone around became increasingly depressed. It wasn't until he was in touch with his own resistance towards being good that any kind of change or breakthrough could take place. Initially he felt guilty from his resistance towards being the good boy. His resistance didn't fit his perception of his use value as the good son. But it was precisely in feeling his hostility that some kind of breakthrough in self-understanding could take place. Shortly we shall return to this subject of valuing experiences not because of their use value but simply because they are what they are.

Our Need to Hurry and Get Things Done. We live in an age of microwaves, instant tea, instant coffee, instant zen, quick weight loss, fast-food restaurants, drive-through banks, and drive-in churches. We encourage people to be brief and to the point in communication, to say what they have to say. We are annoyed when people ramble and take up our time ("I haven't got all day, you know!"). We operate on clock time: two minutes for the water to boil, two hours to develop the film, one and a half hours by plane from Milwaukee to New York, a twenty-minute drive to work. And we are frustrated with delays: waiting an extra twenty minutes for the bus, a five-hour delay at an airport. It seems, even in our age of instants, we are in an even greater hurry to get things done.

Our hope that we'll get through changes as quickly as possible turns to despair as we wait and wait and wonder if we'll ever be able to get on with our lives. "How long do I have to wait before I get over the divorce? How long must I go on hurting over the loss of my wife?" "Did you say it takes years to get through this crisis? Oh no!" Transitions are not governed by clock time. They are not programmable like microwaves. Significant transitions involve deep changes in our attitudes towards ourselves, others, God. And these breakthroughs are like giving birth and being born. Induced prematurely, they can end up being disastrous. Unfortunately, no one can predict exactly how long a transition will last. But our present cultural context makes it difficult for us to stay with the sometimes protracted process leading to a breakthrough.

Clinging to the Present. Being aware of and available to the present is desirable. Holding on to the present is not. "Clinging to the present" and "being aware" are not the same thing. When we are aware, we are open to receiving and letting go, whereas when we cling, we receive but won't let go. It doesn't matter how painful the holding becomes, we continue holding on. For example, people hold on to one another in marriages that have long since soured because an uncertain future without one's spouse seems far worse than their present unhappy relationship. They might continue to heap mental and even physical abuse on one another because they fear letting go of the present.

Clinging to the present might also mean that we construe or interpret our world through biases that never permit reexamination. This group is lazy, that group is greedy, every man is out for himself, and it's a dog-eat-dog world! Or the way I believe in God is the *only* way to believe. Being available to all of our experiences means recognizing that any point of view is limited precisely because it is one view among many. Fortunately, many breakthroughs are breakthroughs that introduce us to new perspectives. But the exceptional strength of a bias might also prevent the new point of view from emerging.

The way in which we breathe helps us understand the difference between clinging and being available to the present. When we breathe deeply and naturally, we freely inhale and exhale, receiving and letting go. If we are nervous, however, our breathing becomes erratic—inhalations become more like gaspings. We are fearful that what we had received so easily and naturally we shall no longer receive. So we momentarily hold on to what we have until we can trust the process again.

Facilitating a Contemplative Attitude

Having identified some attitudes that make it difficult to be available to our experience, it might be helpful to remind ourselves what the goal in going through a transition is and isn't. It isn't wiggling through an uncomfortable mess to a liberating end point called a breakthrough. Rather, it is becoming one with the process of wiggling itself. Process, not progress, is the important word here.

The kind of attitude we need to develop towards our transitional experiences is contemplative. A contemplative stance is a simple, nonjudgmental presence towards experience. Being nonjudgmental means not categorizing what we are going through as either bad or good. It even means that when we do observe ourselves labeling certain thoughts, feelings, inclinations, intuitions,or fantasies as good or bad, we do not compound the problem by judging our own judging as good or bad. Frequently people not only get angry or impatient with themselves; they are highly judgmental towards themselves for being angry or impatient.

Lest there be any misunderstanding, being contemplative doesn't mean our tendencies to become angry or anxious or impatient become magically serene and controlled. Rather, it means that we become increasingly aware of and available to what we experience without being overwhelmed or possessed by our emotions and feelings. Enhancing the awareness of self and others rather than being even more judgmental of self and others is the contemplative's goal.

Being available to our feelings but not overwhelmed by them requires detachment. Detachment doesn't mean being aloof or distant or unconcerned. It means we are present to but not identified with a feeling, a fantasy, a mood, a person. If we are so identified with our feelings or caught up in another's feelings and emotions, then we speak of ourselves as being attached rather than detached. The simple presence to what we are experiencing requires detachment, not attachment. The therapist's attitude towards a client might be helpful in illuminating the meaning of detachment. The psychotherapist needs to be aware of his or her client's feelings and moods. But if the therapist is swept up and identifies with the client's feelings then the therapist loses all objectivity. The needs of the therapist interfere with the therapist's being available to the client.

Similarly, an actor playing Hamlet needs to be available to the words, moods, feelings, and actions the role requires. But he cannot be so identified with them that he thinks he is Hamlet. The actor has simultaneously to be and not be Hamlet. This requires both availability and detachment. Paradoxically, the actor needs to be engaged and disengaged in performing the role of Hamlet. The contemplative's attitude is also paradoxical. Immersed but not lost in what is happening inside and outside the self, the contemplative is intensely alive to the breaking points in the transition.

We have considered five attitudes that make it difficult to value transitions. We can be too future-directed and too concerned about controlling our future. Our pragmatic orientation precludes us from valuing persons, places, things, or activities in and for themselves so that we notice only what is useful, that is, see the other in terms of functionality.

The hurried and harried pace that frequently governs whatever we are doing prevents us from fully entering into the present moment. We also find ourselves holding on to the present, attempting to capture it or freeze it in time.

We might be able to modify these attitudes, but not by any major assault on them or an aggressive agenda to eradicate them. Attempts to change them directly would simply reinforce them. Having a new agenda to be contemplative invites a new way of being pragmatic (e.g., meditating in order to be more peaceful), as well as a new way of being programmatic (e.g., a six-week plan with a detailed description of what and when something is to happen). One becomes fixed intently on what is supposed to happen to oneself with all the preconceptions of how one is to turn out.

Though we cannot begin to change these attitudes directly without at the same time reinforcing them, we can do so indirectly. We can become aware of factors in any activity that dispose us towards being contemplative, that urge us gently towards a more contemplative attitude. And what might those factors be?

Someone who has extensively researched and written on the factors that are present in the contemplative experiences is Mihalyi Csikszentmihalyi. He refers to them as "flow" experiences, "the state in which people are so involved in an activity that nothing else seems to matter; the experience itself is so enjoyable that people will do it even at great cost for the sheer sake of doing it."[2] Flow describes "seemingly effortless movement."[3]

These experiences are as varied as singing, mountain climbing, playing the piano, dancing, carrying on an animated conversation, and meditating. Csikszentmihalyi writes that when people reflect on how it feels when their experience is most positive, they mention at least one and often eight components in the flow experience.

> First, the experience usually occurs when we confront tasks we have a chance of completing. Second, we must be able to concentrate on what we are doing. Third and fourth, the concentration is usually possible because the task undertaken has clear goals and provides immediate feedback. Fifth, one acts with a deep but effortless involvement that removes from awareness the worries and frustrations of everyday life. Sixth, enjoyable experiences allow people to exercise a sense of control over their actions. Seventh, concern for the self disappears, yet paradoxically the sense of self emerges stronger after the flow experience is over.

Finally, the sense of the duration of time is altered;
hours pass by in minutes, and minutes can stretch
out to seem like hours.[4]

Having identified components in the flow experience,
we are now in a position to observe how these factors contribute indirectly to developing a contemplative attitude during a transition. In many of our transitions, we often feel our
lives are at a standstill. We aren't productive and we can't
seem to get anything accomplished. We feel guilty because
we are wasting time and feeling useless. But we can learn a
valuable lesson from flow experiences. Flow experiences are
self-contained. They provide immediate feedback. We are
rewarded in doing them simply for the joy of it. Here we learn
that meaning and value in life are not restricted to productivity. We can be involved in "useless" activities and still experience them as meaningful. A contemplative "wastes" time
intentionally in prayer and in play. Often it is necessary for us
to go through a transition before we realize that productivity
is a value but not the *only* value in life.

We have already seen that in transitions we frequently
feel we are not in control of our lives. This might be particularly painful to realize if we have been very controlling persons. Yet it is a lesson we need to learn. However, while it is
important that we realize that the chronic need to be in control does not foster a contemplative attitude, this doesn't
mean that *exercising* control is countercontemplative. Csikszentmihalyi makes the point that the flow experience is typ-
ically described as involving a *sense* of control. This sense of
control can contribute to a positive self-concept, which
would be especially welcome during transitions when our
self-esteem tends to be low.

For example, challenges met on the tennis court or on
the dance floor or at a chess game are opportunities for exer-

cising control. However, meeting these challenges doesn't mean that the participants feel like failures because they can't control what happens.

Closely related to the loss of control in transitions is the loss of focus. We find it difficult to focus or concentrate on what we are doing. What had given structure to our lives—roles, status, relationships, work—either is no longer present or no longer meaningful. And where there is no structure there is no order. But if we are engaged in experiences that temporarily introduce order into our chaotic lives, then we are more likely to endure these lengthy periods in which the gradual restructuring of our lives is taking place. Thus, any activity is invaluable if it focuses our energies, challenges but does not exceed our skills to meet the challenges, and gives clear goals and feedback. Such experiences are capable of creating order in consciousness and strengthening the structure of the self.

Finally, activities that require our wholehearted attention in the present moment might help us to be more contemplative during our transitions. Transitions are like forced retreats. We don't ask for these breaks in our lives. They happen. But when they do, we have an opportunity to gain some perspective on where we have been and where we are going. They afford us the opportunity to become more attentive to what is happening in and around us. Flow experiences are exercises in tending the present moment. Even if we are writing in a journal about some past event, we present ourselves fully to that moment. Were it not for our transitions, we might never slow down and take stock of our lives. To experience flow is to be available wherever we are in whatever we are doing.

Flow experiences are certainly not the answer to all of our problems, but they can be helpful in developing a contemplative attitude. The challenges they offer are no greater than our abilities to meet those challenges, and they can be life-giving oases in some often dry stretches of our lives.

Journaling

One activity that many have found especially helpful in becoming more present or available to themselves and to others is keeping a journal. Journaling has much to commend it, not only because it is a potentially contemplative activity but also because it puts us in touch with dimensions of ourselves that ordinarily escape our notice. By sensitizing ourselves to what is taking place within and around us, journaling provides the opportunity of being aware of the breakthrough we are in the process of becoming. For this reason it is appropriate to consider how journaling contributes to developing a contemplative attitude during our transitions. A few concrete suggestions about journaling and resources on journaling follow this reflection.

At the beginning or end of each day, if we sit and write down our thoughts, feelings, and intuitions of the last twenty-four hours, our words become the bridge between the conscious, known side of ourselves and the unconscious, unknown side. We do not aggressively set out to discover what is unknown about ourselves. However, as we give ourselves permission to write whatever needs to be written, we find that our words mirror what is going on inside of us. Better, our words are like midwives, drawing out hidden dimensions of ourselves into the light of day.

Our words are like symbols inasmuch as they both express and embody something of the unknown side of ourselves to ourselves. In any symbol the expression and the embodiment is always partial, since no word or image adequately discloses all there is to know about the unknown. Thus, infinite being is capable of being imaged in a variety of ways, and while some ways are especially honored within a religious tradition (e.g., God as Father), no one image is God. Regarding the words we use in journaling, no one image in a given entry adequately describes all that there is to say about the unknown within ourselves. On one day we might be writing that we're on cloud nine, while on the next we might be in the desert. In both entries our words tell us something about ourselves but never everything. They are important insofar as they enable us to be more aware of the moments of elation as well as those of desolation.

This explanation of the value of journaling as a mirror or as a midwife is itself an attempt to use images to describe the connections between one side of the self and another. In using these or other images, we try to get a better appreciation for something of ourselves that is as much us as our conscious side but much more elusive and obscure to us.

Another image can be helpful in connecting with the inner unknown when we are writing in the journal: the image of a *partner* in dialogue. This partner speaks to us from the depths in and through our words and our thoughts. Exploring partners in dialogue might give us a better insight into our inner other as well as into the value of dialoguing with that partner.

Often we assume that the more mature we are, the more unified we become. And what would this inner unity mean if not being of one mind, one heart, and one voice? Wasn't that the point in distinguishing my voice from *their* voices to achieve a clear understanding of the one, true voice that is mine? Isn't this what we mean when we speak of "getting our act together"? If transitions are times of confusion and upheaval during which we're uncertain who we are and where we're going, wouldn't a successful resolution mean some one voice was finally taking control?

But what if maturing means an increased awareness of and a willingness to listen to and dialogue with the many voices of the self that speak from within? What if the chaotic transitions are the opportune times when this multifaceted self that had been ignored can no longer be silenced and demands a hearing? Would a breakthrough in a transition then mean we were learning to appreciate the variety of ways in which the self speaks? And would we be more likely to view this richness as a blessing than a curse?

If all this talk about the self sounds strange, perhaps it will become clearer if we pause and ask ourselves what this self is with which we need to dialogue. Isn't it true that we always seem to regard the self as another person? We address it and refer to it as an inner other. For example, sometimes we don't get along with ourselves. And what do we say? "I don't like myself," or "I can't stand myself," or "I hate myself." Of course, if we feel this negatively toward ourselves, then we say, "I can't go on living with myself." At other times the way we talk betrays an uncertainty about the partner we call the self. We say, "I'm afraid of myself," or "I don't know if I can trust myself," or "I don't know what got into me."

There are times when we can't even find ourselves. So we say, "Gee, I'm out of touch with myself," or "I'm beside myself." What's frightening is when we can't seem to control ourselves, as in "I lost control of myself," or "I don't know what happened to myself—I just started crying!" Of course, it isn't always frightening. The unexpected is sometimes welcome, and we say, "I surprised myself! I didn't know I had it in me."

On the other hand, nothing surprising happens, and we say, "I am bored with myself," followed by "And I don't want to go home and be by myself." But we have every right to be proud of ourselves when we say, "I've got to go and work this thing out by myself," and return elated because "I figured it out by myself!" Then we don't mind the quiet. "I enjoy being by myself. I really like myself!"

Finally, we all know that there is only one other self that we will be with until the day we die—my self. So we say with a certain urgency, "I've got to be able to live with myself," and that means at times, "I've got to confront myself," or "I need to take stock of myself."

The self we so often glibly assume to know is a partner in dialogue. It can be as unpredictable, maddening, frightening, friendly, and elusive as any person we know—friend, lover, or spouse. Given the range of feelings and attitudes we bring to the self, no wonder it's such a challenge to discover who this self is.

Learning who this self is, however, is not our sole task. We cannot know that self unless we enlist its support to help us. Partners are in dialogue with one another; they are mutually supportive. One partner doesn't carry the burden of the relationship, and in the present instance this means "I" alone can't shoulder the burden of acceptance. My partner—that is, my self and I—both bear that responsibility. And how might we do this?

I spoke about being out of touch with myself. This means being out of touch with moods, fantasies, feelings, attitudes. Certainly it is important that we reach out and touch this dimension of the self. But we also need to give our self permission to touch *us*. We must permit these feelings, moods, and the like to be. We don't force them; we receive them. We get close to them, and they get close to us.

Sometimes we try to figure things out, and we are exhausted. *We* do the trying, and *we* do the working—to no avail! Maybe if we rest, our self will come to our assistance with clues, suggestions, and hints. These are the creative moments when we discover that solutions to problems surface without our having done anything at all to produce them. We know the wisdom of that self when we say, "I think I'm trying too hard to solve this problem; I'll put it on the back burner!" To "put a problem on the back burner" is another way of speaking about the self as the creative agent that provides insights not available on the front burner.

Then there are the times when we are afraid or bored to be by ourselves. In these instances we seem to regard that self as an inner alien or as an enemy. We try to hide from this self through distractions—playing loud music, never permitting ourselves to be alone, or whatever. Maybe if we quiet down and get close to that self, we will discover that being alone with our self isn't all that bad. Moments of solitude can be refreshing.

We have all said or done things that seemed out of character. We blurted out angry words, or we sobbed uncontrollably over some insignificant issue. Perhaps we had long neglected getting close to that self and finally noticed how it was hurting. Like any other hurting person, when the self hurts, it needs to be noticed. And if the self has been unduly neglected, it will seek attention in any way it can.

The burden of accepting ourselves is relieved considerably if we realize that we are involved in a partnership. We are called to reach out to our self, but this self reaches out to us as well. Realizing this give and take, we can be more open to those moments when we don't need to do anything to experience acceptance. It just happens! We feel at one with our self—there is a genuine communion in which we experience being partners.

As we have discovered, the experience of breaking away is one of differentiating what is us from what is not us. And this differentiation is both interpersonal and intrapersonal. We need to distinguish who we are from the outer others (family, friends, society), as well as from the others as they have been internalized in the scripts or voices we carry in our heads. However, we also need to identify and dialogue with the many dimensions of the self that have their own voices within us and seek a hearing. Our respect for this inner pluralism is simultaneously a recognition that maturing means unity in diversity rather than the simple-minded reduction of all voices to one.

Given this explanation why the image of partners in dialogue is helpful in imaging the relation of ourselves to the unknown in ourselves, what are helpful guidelines in keeping a journal and preventing our writing from becoming simply an academic exercise?

1. We honor ourselves and what we are doing by finding a time and place which can be for us a sacred time and space for ritualizing our activity. Writing in a journal is our own liminal experience of being who we are apart from our own and others' expectations of who or what we ought to be.

2. In writing we need not be concerned about correct spelling, grammatical correctness, penmanship. When we write in a journal, we are writing for ourselves.

3. We might discover as we write that we are writing as if someone were looking over our shoulder and reading everything we wrote. It is a revelation to discover as we write how much we are governed by what others might think or feel about us. This is apparent as we hurriedly erase a word, sentence, or paragraph and mutter, "I didn't mean that! How could I?" What we have written might seem too harsh, vindictive, or angry, too affirming, caring, or nurturing. Let the writing stand as it is! If there is a need to qualify what has been written, we can add the qualifiers. The disclosures in our writing about what we feel we can or cannot write, what we wished we had or had not written, the words we inadvertently use, are as

important as what we set out to write. These are soul words, not polite table talk meant to impress others!

4. What we also want to note is the speed and intensity with which we write, the pressure we apply on the pen as we write, the need to repeat or linger over words we've written, the varied sizes of the letters in our written words. All of this tells us about our feelings, moods, longings. The words are ourselves invested mightily in what we are doing.

5. We ought to reread aloud whatever we have written and hear in our voice the feeling we had not gotten in the writing. Hearing ourselves is yet another way to hear our souls as the soul seeks expression.

Occasionally we need to remind ourselves that being present and available is what journaling is about. The purpose in journaling is not external to the exercise. We aren't writing to get better, to be more self-actualized, to solve problems, or to make more money. Process, not progress, is everything. Where we are going is where we are!

In our transitions we have the experience but often miss the meaning (T.S. Eliot). In this chapter we have identified attitudes that inhibit the discovery of meaning as well as the attitude that enables us to find it in transitions. We have noted that we cannot develop a contemplative attitude in any aggressive, goal-oriented approach that draws our attention from the experiences themselves. What we can do is dispose ourselves towards being contemplative by being mindful of those factors in flow experiences. By reflecting on the times when some or all of these factors have been operative and by engaging in activities in which they once more might be operative, we can become more contemplative.

An exercise like journaling can sensitize us to the transformative experiences that easily go unnoticed when we are tending them. Close attention to the present moment, especially to those times of transformation, is what we mean when we say the attitude is contemplative.

Conclusion

We can conclude this book on transitions by reflecting on one of the journey stories we find in the gospel of Matthew. I am referring to the journey of the Magi (Mt 2:1–12). Like so many other journey stories, this story has a threefold structure. The Magi leave the known, travel through the unknown, and then reach their destination. However, this journey story varies from others because of the special star that guides them to their destination. We can imagine them following the star, occasionally losing sight of it, rediscovering it, and finally being led to the stable by it. The story mirrors much of what we have noted about our own transitions.

On our own journeys we are also guided by a star. The star is our dream, our ambition, our aspiration. It is our vision of who or what we shall become and how we shall shine. Our destination is the fulfillment of our heart's desire. However, it isn't entirely clear how we might find fulfillment. The object of our heart's desire is shaped considerably by our needs and expectations. We have our illusions. "One day I'll do this and the next day this will happen. All I need to do is study here, or marry this person, or get this job, and it will work out as I had planned." "It" will take shape. We do not realize that there is something self-aggrandizing about how "my" star is going to shine.

But neither we nor the Magi control the course of the star. They have to cross deserts where the watering holes are few and far between. Cloudy skies might hide the star in endless dark nights that leave them feeling lost. Or possibly the star itself might no longer seem to be the star that initially preceded them on their journey. We, too, find ourselves crossing deserts where we are not sure of our direction. And during these times we become disillusioned because our star seems to have disappeared. Then we are sorely tempted to conclude that there was no reality to our dream, our star. We are not the successful writer or lover or parent we had imagined we would become. Or maybe we are successful only to discover that there was more in the promise than in the reality.

Transitions in which we cross the desert are times for becoming aware of who or what shapes our star. And often how we shine has little to do with our illusions of either what it means to shine or how it will happen.

During these times we might also become aware that pursuing this star is not something we can do alone. We do it by accompanying and being accompanied by others. This is *communitas,* bonding with others on the level of our shared humanity. This insight might lead to the star emerging from behind the clouds—not mine, but ours. But what emerges is not like the star of our beginnings. It shines but not as it had originally shone.

But what of our destination? We know that this star led the Magi to a stable where a helpless naked baby lay. Through our transitions our star brings us to the realization that how we shine has nothing to do with how we will it to shine. Self-aggrandizement has no place at the manger. We shine in simply being who we are to one another as the child was to the Magi.

If we have anything to rejoice in it is this simple presence that we can be and are called to be for one another. The journey does not end at the stable because it needs to be undertaken over and over. Our transitions will always play an important part in discovering and rediscovering who we are alone and together as we follow our star.

Notes

Introduction

1. Ann Morrow Lindbergh, *Gift from the Sea* (New York: Vintage, 1978), p. 88.

Chapter 1

1. James Baldwin, *Nobody Knows My Name* (New York: Dial Press, 1961), p. 117.

2. Frances Wickes, *The Inner World of Choice* (Boston: Sigo Press, 1988), pp. 117, 118.

3. Kegan used the expressions the "socializing mind" and the "self-authorizing mind" in his lecture "Respecting Our Complexity" at the John Neumann Summer Institute, Hales Corners, WI, 1994. In his book *The Evolving Self* (Cambridge: Harvard University Press, 1982), he writes of the "interpersonal self" and the "institutional self," but in his last book, *In Over Our Heads: The Mental Demands of Modern Life* (Cambridge: Harvard University Press, 1994), he writes of the "third" and "fourth" orders of consciousness.

4. Kegan, *The Evolving Self,* pp. 103 ff.

Chapter 2

1. Robert Moore and Douglas Gillette, *The Magician Within* (San Francisco: Harper, 1993), p. 108.

2. Victor Turner, "Betwixt and Between: The Liminal Period in Rites of Passage," in *Betwixt & Between: Patterns of Masculine and Feminine Initiation* (LaSalle, IL: Open Court, 1987), p. 9.

3. I am indebted to James Hillman's essay "Betrayal," in

Loose Ends (New York: Spring Publications, 1975), for this list of reactions with the exception of the one on shame.

4. John Patton, *Is Human Forgiveness Possible?* (Nashville: Abingdon), p. 186.

5. Peter D. Baird, *Forgiveness, New York Times,* July 7, 1991, p. 8.

Chapter 3

1. Dante, *Inferno,* ll. 1–3.

2. Lesley Hazleton, *The Right to Feel Bad* (New York: Ballantine Books), pp. 11 ff.

3. Peter Marris, *Loss and Change* (London: Routledge & Kegan, 1986), p. 33.

4. Janice Wood Wetzel, *Clinical Handbook of Depression* (New York: Gardner Press, 1984), p. 284.

5. Jean Baker Miller, *Toward a New Psychology of Women* (Boston: Beacon Press), pp. 49 ff.

6. Wetzel, pp. 287, 288.

7. Kegan, *The Evolving Self,* pp. 267–273.

8. David H. Rosen, *Transforming Depression* (New York: Tarcher-Putnam, 1993), pp. 61–84.

9. Moore and Gillette, *The Magician Within,* p. 124.

10. Ibid., pp. 124, 125.

11. Ibid., p. 108.

12. Thomas Moore, *Care of the Soul* (San Francisco: HarperCollins, 1992), p. 139.

13. Ibid., p. 142.

Chapter 4

1. R. D. Laing, *The Divided Self* (New York: Pantheon, 1960).

2. J. Randall Nichols, *Ending Marriage; Keeping Faith* (New York: Crossroad, 1991), pp. 9 ff.

3. Rainer Maria Rilke, *Letters to a Young Poet* (New York: Random House, 1985), pp. 34, 35.

4. Kegan, *The Evolving Self,* p. 107.

5. Ibid., pp. 116–132.

6. Robert Wuthnow, *Sharing the Journey* (New York: Free Press, 1994) p. 31.

7. Ibid., pp. 359, 360.

8. Ibid., p. 64.

9. Victor Turner, *The Ritual Process* (Chicago: Aldine, 1969) pp. 95 ff.

Chapter 5

1. James E. Dittes, *The Male Predicament* (New York: Harper & Row, 1985), p. 57.

2. Ibid., p. 54.

3. Sam Gill, "Disenchantment," in *Parabola,* Summer 1976.

4. Quoted in Matthew Fox, *Breakthrough* (New York: Doubleday, 1980), pp. 304, 305.

5. Robert Kegan, "There the Dance: Religious Dimensions of a Developmental Framework," in *Toward Moral and Religious Maturity* (Morristown: Silver Burdett, 1980) p. 421.

6. Ibid., p. 419.

7. Urban T. Holmes, *Ministry and Imagination* (New York: Seabury, 1981), p. 121.

8. Ibid., pp. 121, 122.

9. Evelyn Underhill, *Mysticism* (New York: World, 1955) p. 386.

10. Quoted in William James, *The Varieties of Religious Experience* (New York: New American Library, 1958), pp. 130, 132.

11. Ibid., pp. 130, 132.

12. Ibid., p. 132.

13. Ibid., p. 154.

14. Ibid., p. 154.

Chapter 6

1. Nikos Kazantzakis, *Zorba the Greek.*

2. Mihalyi Csikszentmihalyi, *Flow: The Psychology of Optimal Experience* (New York: Harper & Row, 1990), p. 4.

3. Ibid., p. 54.

4. Ibid., p. 49.

Bibliography

Alexander, Bobby C. 1991. *Victor Turner Revisited*. Atlanta: Scholars Press.

Baldwin, James. 1961. *Nobody Knows My Name*. New York: Dial Press.

Bridges, William. 1991. *Managing Transitions: Making the Most of Change*. Reading, MA: Addison-Wesley.

——. 1990. *Transitions*. Reading, MA: Addison-Wesley.

Cameron, Julia. 1992. *The Artist's Way*. New York: Putnam.

Csikszentmihalyi, Mihaly. 1990. *Flow: The Psychology of Optimal Experience*. New York: Harper & Row.

Dittes, James E. 1985. *The Male Predicament*. New York: Harper & Row.

Duff, Kat. 1993. *The Alchemy of Illness*. New York: Pantheon.

Fitzgerald, Constance, O.C.D. 1995. "Desolation as Dark Night." *The Way Supplement;* Spring, 82.

——. "Impasse and the Dark Night." In *Living with Apocalypse,* ed. Tilden H. Edwards. San Francisco: Harper & Row.

Fox, Matthew. 1980. *Breakthrough: Meister Eckhart's Creation Spirituality in New Translation*. New York: Doubleday.

Gerzon, Mark. 1992. *Coming into Our Own*. New York: Delacorte.

Gill, Sam. 1976. "Disenchantment." *Parabola,* Summer.

Gutmann, David. 1987. *Reclaimed Powers: Towards a*

New Psychology of Men and Women in Later Life. New York: Basic Books.

Harding, M. Esther. 1985. *The Value and Meaning of Depression.* New York: Analytical Psychology Club of New York, Inc.

Hazleton, Lesley. 1985. *The Right to Feel Bad.* New York: Ballantine.

Hillman, James. 1975. "Betrayal." In *Loose Ends.* New York: Spring Publications.

Holmes, Urban T. 1981. *Ministry and Imagination.* New York: Seabury Press.

Hudson, Frederic M. 1991. *The Adult Years: Mastering the Art of Self-Renewal.* San Francisco: Jossey-Bass Inc.

Jack, Dana Crowley. 1991. *Silencing the Self: Women and Depression.* Cambridge: Harvard University Press.

James, William. 1958. *The Varieties of Religious Experience.* New York: New American Library.

Johnson, Robert. 1986. *Inner Work.* New York: Harper & Row.

Kazantzakis, Nikos. 1971. *Zorba the Greek.* New York: Simon and Schuster.

Kegan, Robert. 1982. *The Evolving Self.* Cambridge: Harvard University Press.

———. 1994. *In over Our Heads: The Mental Demands of Modern Life.* Cambridge: Harvard University Press.

———. 1980. "There the Dance: Religious Dimensions of a Developmental Framework." In *Toward Moral and Religious Maturity.* Morristown, NJ: Silver Burdett.

Kohut, Heinz. 1971. *The Analysis of the Self.* New York: International Universities Press.

———. 1977. *The Restoration of the Self.* New York: International Universities Press.

Laing, R. D. 1960. *The Divided Self.* New York: Pantheon.

Levinson, Daniel. 1978. *The Seasons of a Man's Life.* New York: Knopf.

Leech, Kenneth. 1985. *Experiencing God: Theology as Spirituality.* New York: Harper & Row.

Lindbergh, Anne Morrow. 1978. *Gift from the Sea.* New York: Vintage.

Mahdi, Louise C., Nancy Geyer Christopher, and Michael Meade, eds. 1996. *Crossroads: The Quest for Contemporary Rites of Passage.* Lasalle, Illinois: *Open Court.*

Mahdi, Louise C., Steven Foster, and Meredith Little, eds. 1987. *Betwixt & Between: Patterns of Masculine and Feminine Initiation.* LaSalle, IL: Open Court.

Marris, Peter. 1986. *Loss and Change.* London: Routledge & Kegan Paul.

May, Gerald. 1988. *Addiction and Grace.* New York: Harper & Row.

Meadow, Mary J. "The Dark Side of Mysticism: Depression and the 'Dark Night.'" *Pastoral Psychology* 33 Winter 1984,104–125.

Miller, Alice. 1981. *The Drama of the Gifted Child.* New York: Harper Colophon.

Miller, Jean Baker. 1986. *Toward a New Psychology of Women.* 2nd ed. Boston: Beacon Press.

Miller, William A. 1981. *Make Friends with Your Shadow.* Minneapolis: Augsburg.

Moore, Robert, and Douglas Gillette. 1993. *The Magician Within.* San Francisco: Harper.

Moore, Thomas. 1992. *Care of the Soul.* San Francisco: HarperCollins.

Nichols, J. Randall. 1991. *Ending Marriage, Keeping Faith.* New York: Crossroad.

Papineau, Andre. 1989. Introduction to *Biblical Blues.* San José: Resource Publications.

———. 1988. Introduction to *Breakthrough: Tales of Conversion.* San José: Resource Publications.

Patton, John. 1985. *Is Human Forgiveness Possible?* Nashville: Abingdon Press.

Raphael, Ray. 1988. *The Men from the Boys: Rites of Passage in Male America.* Lincoln: University of Nebraska Press.

Real, Terrence. 1997. *I Don't Want to Talk About It: Overcoming the Secret of Male Depression.* New York: Scribner.

Rilke, Rainer Maria. 1984. *Letters to a Young Poet.* New York: Random House.

Rosen, David H. 1993. *Transforming Depression.* New York: Tarcher-Putnam.

Sammon, Sean D. 1983. *Growing Pains in Ministry.* Mystic, CT: Twenty-third Publications.

Sliker, Gretchen. 1992. *Multiple Mind.* Boston: Shambhala.

Tennov, Dorothy. 1980. *Love and Limerence: The Experience of Being in Love.* Scarborough Books.

Turner, Victor. 1969. *The Ritual Process.* Chicago: Aldine.

———. 1972. "Passages, Margins, and Poverty: Religious Symbols of Communitas." *Worship* 46.

Trafford, Abigail. 1982. *Crazy Times: Surviving Divorce.* New York: Harper & Row.

Underhill, Evelyn. 1955. *Mysticism.* New York: World.

Van Kaam, Adrian. 1987. "Addiction: Counterfeit of Religious Experience." *Studies in Formative Spirituality* 7, 243–45.

Viorst, Judith. 1986. *Necessary Losses*. New York: Simon and Schuster.

Wetzel, Janice Wood. 1984. *Clinical Handbook of Depression*. New York: Gardner Press.

Whitehead, Evelyn and James D. 1979. *Christian Life Patterns*. New York: Doubleday.

Wickes, Frances. 1988. *The Inner World of Choice*. Boston: Sigo Press.

Wuthnow, Robert. 1994. *Sharing the Journey*. New York: Free Press.